THE DIRECT PATH:

A User Guide

GREG GOODE

NON-DUALITY PRESS

UNITED KINGDOM

The Direct Path

First English edition published February 2012 by Non-Duality Press

Non-Duality Press is an Imprint of

 new**harbinger**publications, inc.

5674 Shattuck Avenue • Oakland CA 94609 • USA
800-748-6273 • fax 510-652-5472
www.newharbinger.com

ISBN: 978-1-908664-02-0
www.newharbinger.com

Acknowledgments

I am indebted to Colin M. Turbayne (1916 – 2006), whose profound insights into non-objectivity constitute a powerful Western version of the Direct Path. He also demonstrated to me that inquiry can be a living thing. I would also like to thank Richard Rorty (1931 – 2007), anti-dualist and philosophical renegade, for his liberating presentation of irony.

I'd like to thank Francis Lucille and Watkins Books for introducing me to the writings of Shri Atmananda (1883 – 1959). I have never met Shri Atmananda, but Francis and Watkins Books provided a living context for his teachings.

Last but not least, I wish to thank Dr. Tamara Vyshkina and Dr. Tomas Sander for their excellent editorial assistance. They nurtured the text with great care, which was guided by their linguistic skill and a deep familiarity with the Direct Path. Any errors or bloopers that remain are due to Greg.

Greg Goode

OVERVIEW

ANALYTICAL TABLE OF CONTENTS

EXPERIMENTS

INTRODUCTION

This is a set of experiential tips and experiments for the Direct Path. What I mean by the "Direct Path" is the set of self-inquiry teachings attributed by Nitya Tripta to Shri Atmananda Krishna Menon and later elaborated upon by Jean Klein, John Levy, Alexander Smit, Philip Renard, Francis Lucille and Rupert Spira. This book can also be considered a user guide or "missing manual" to my own **Standing as Awareness**.

This book consists of a set of experiments, with explanatory text. The book's purpose is to deeply investigate many different aspects of experience, including sensation, perception, bodily feeling and motion, waking and sleeping, emotion, attention, thought, rationality, and the sense of being a single, global, unlimited witness of all that arises. What we discover in every case is that there are actually no independent objects experienced at any time. There is never any separation or otherness, but simply love, openness, clarity, sweetness, awareness – in short, your true nature itself. This approach is often called a "tattvopadesha," a sequential, logically connected presentation of the teaching from beginning to end.

How To Use This Book

There are several ways to use this book, and you can mix and match as you please.

- You can read through from the beginning to the end, the same way you would read any other book on nonduality. You can include the experiments or skip them.

▪ You can do a "slow read." This is akin to the classic contemplative reading or "lectio divina" of the mystics. It is when you savor the flavor of the words and passages, immersing yourself in the sweetness, as awareness speaks to you. Here, too, you can include the experiments or skip them.

▪ You can focus on the experiments, starting at the beginning and working your way through. The experiments have been organized from the concrete to the abstract. They all represent identifiable barriers that come up for people as they do self-inquiry.

▪ You can pick and choose the experiments. You would do this by using the Table of Contents and Index to find topics and issues you are interested in.

Who Is This Book For?

This book is for anyone who encounters a sticking point in their inquiry. That topic may well be covered here. In fact, most of the topics were included because they have been questions raised in people's inquiry. This book is also for anyone who:

- Wishes to further explore the sweetness of having fallen in love with awareness.

- Feels drawn to know the truth of their being and the nature of the world.

- Wishes to explore the world of their experience to discover what lies at its core.

Love

> 1. *You do not know anything but yourself.*
> 2. *You do not love anything but yourself.*
> *So both knowledge and love have yourself as their*
> *object. Therefore, you are pure Knowledge and Love.*

Notes on Spiritual Discourses of Shri Atmananda,
Vol. 1, p. 47, Note #80. [1]

In everyday terms, the goal of inquiry in the Direct Path is to integrate the head and the heart in unity. In this unity, knowledge and love are flipsides on a 45 rpm record of infinite thinness. Knowledge is love distilled by clarity. Love is knowledge pervaded by sweetness. In this clarity there is no cold intellectualizing or blind sentimentality.

Love itself is transformational. If one doesn't fall in love with anything along the way, not even a little bit, then it will be hard for experience to feel sweet. What kinds of things can one fall in love with? Candidates include awareness, the teaching, the teacher, a book, Being, the universe, God, Krishna, Jesus, Buddha, or anything that represents the goal of your inquiry.

In practical terms, love and knowledge enhance each other. Love provides sweetness and ease to knowledge. Knowledge accelerates and broadens the focus of love. They meet in reality.

Love helps your understanding like this: when you do devotional or bhakti-yoga activities, your heart opens and the realizations in your inquiry are smoother and easier. There are fewer sticking points along the way, and it seems like less "work." All experience becomes more savory and fragrant.

Inquiry opens your heart and broadens your love like this: when you do inquiry, something uncanny happens to the object of your love. It stops seeming like a distinct object whether gross or subtle. It is not experienced as different from you, and it begins to spread out and become everything. You no longer have to look in one particular direction to find your beloved. Your beloved and its sweetness are everywhere you turn.

Nondual Inquiry And Conventional Therapies

The Direct Path is a route of nondual inquiry that leads to the recognition of yourself as awareness, beauty and love. It is not a goal of the Direct Path to transform you into a person to whom only pleasant things happen. Instead of this phenomenal goal, the Direct Path has a deeper, more radical goal. The Direct Path reveals awareness to be the very nature of the person. Awareness is prior to the person, so it can't be possessed by the person. Nondual inquiry seeks to discover and clarify this nature. In doing so, it subjects the very perspective of the person to deep and radical scrutiny.

Sometimes nondual paths are described as freeing one from suffering. They succeed admirably at this, but not by giving you more favorable experiences. Nondual inquiry does not work by retaining the person but eradicating the suffering. It is much more thorough than that. What happens through nondual inquiry is that you come experientially to realize the truth of yourself as awareness, brilliant clarity and global love, in which there is neither suffering nor personhood.

People often wonder whether there is any contradiction between nondual inquiry and conventional therapies. Because nondual inquiry does not seek to improve the person, it has no quarrel with conventional therapies. The goals are different. Modalities such as psychiatry and psychotherapy seek to improve the person through techniques that engender a healthy, flourishing person. Psychiatry may even prescribe medicine. Improving the person is a broad goal also shared by medicine, dentistry, physical fitness, exercise and education. Because a person can participate in more than one activity in life, nondual inquiry does not see itself as having an either/or relationship with these other activities. One can combine nondual inquiry with any of these activities. Of course, nondualism submits the notion of the "person" to radical scrutiny, but this does not mean that one must stop going to the dentist. One can very well participate in these other activities without taking their goals and models as literal, objective truths. In many cases, each activity helps the other.

The various therapies have various goals, corresponding with the needs of the person. A person may want to do nondual inquiry, but may be blocked by severe physical or mental pain. In such a case, the "direct path" to the relief from that pain is not nondual inquiry at all, but physical or mental therapy. And just as a person does not expect nondual inquiry to alleviate a toothache, one would not expect dental therapy to be the key to realizing the truth of the self. It is much more "direct" to follow the most efficient route to the goal at hand, while allowing the goals to assist each other.

The Main Problem

The main problem that self-inquiry addresses is what Nitya Tripta's **Notes on Spiritual Discourses of Shri Atmananda** calls "wrong identification." In other words, we take ourselves to be something we're not. We think, feel and act as though we are a body or a mind or a combination of both, whereas the truth is that we are awareness. It normally seems as though we are some sort of particular object, whereas we are actually the witnessing awareness to which these objects appear. We are not the objects seen, but the seeingness itself.

Traditional Advaita-Vedanta gives this wrong identification the unwieldy name, "mutual superimposition of the self and the non-self." In mutual superimposition, we mix up the subject and objects. We take one thing as another. Awareness is the *subject* but we treat it as an *object*, such as when we think that awareness can be seen or localized or personalized. On the other hand, we treat (some) *objects* as though they are the *subject*, such as when we think that a body or mind can see or apprehend.

It is inevitable that this mix-up leads to suffering. Even though we are awareness, if we take ourselves as some kind of object like a body or mind, then we feel limited, impermanent and vulnerable. We feel we can disappear like other objects. Our pleasures, passions and possessions are temporary and doomed to vanish or fade away. Our lives as humans seem all too short. We seem bound to suffer bad fortune, guilt, shame, cruelty, pain, poverty, disease and death. These things are naturally expected to happen to objects. So if we are an object, it is inevitable to think that these things will happen to us.

But awareness, our true nature, isn't limited, personal, impermanent or temporary. It is THAT to which objects (even universes) appear. It is THAT in which they arise and fall. The person is an object, so the person comes and goes. Awareness can't come and go since it is THAT to which coming-and-going appears! There is no fear or suffering here.

Your investigation into your direct experience will reveal that all these objects aren't really objects anyway, but that they have been aware-ness all along. Thus, all the issues of identification and all the issues of the subject vs. objects – all of it will collapse into sweetness and clarity.

The Direct Path's Solution

The solution to wrong identification is "right identification."[2] Right iden-tification is basically "no identification." As awareness we don't need to think that we are anything at all. The very need for thinking we are something drops away. The result is just *being*, as opposed to *being something.*

Of course, when one begins nondual inquiry, one usually goes through a stage in which one does explicitly identify with awareness. It seems like a new identification in place of the old one. This is quite natu-ral, and it can even seem like putting on a new and strange new suit of clothes. But this sense of strangeness diminishes; nondual teachings give us lots of different kinds of pointers that allow us to discover how being awareness is not new or strange at all, but perfectly natural. You get to the point where there is direct, intuitive, nonconceptual experience of being awareness. When this is deeply and directly seen, it cuts through identification with objects. It short-circuits the mutual superimposition and wrong identifications.

Once you know yourself as awareness, there is no need to take yourself as anything else. The sense of explicitly identifying with anything, *even with awareness*, drops away. Standing as awareness, being awareness will be your reality. Even if it seemed odd when you first encountered nondual teachings, it's perfectly natural. Standing as awareness isn't even anything you *do*. It is your natural state, and when this is directly seen, the world of experience will lovingly and smilingly confirm your stand at every moment.

How Does The Direct Path Work?

There are many ways that Direct Path teachers point to your nature as awareness. The primary tool is direct investigation into your experience. This is a general category which can have many entry points. Besides standing as awareness, they include:

- Investigating the world, body and mind; the result is that they are revealed as awareness and not as objects at all.

- Investigating deep sleep and sleeping knowingly.[3]

- Investigating the witness aspect of experience.

- Cultivating the intense feeling that you are not the doer or enjoyer.

- Cultivating the conviction that knowledge and happiness are your nature.

Western Direct-Path teachers place more emphasis on the body, science, love and psychological factors than one finds in traditional Advaita-Vedanta teachings. This is a natural consequence of the teaching making its way from one culture to another. In Western gatherings and teaching sessions you will see activities such as yoga, perceptual exercises, body-sensing – all of which help one realize that the body is not the container of awareness or the source of sentience, but a set of objects like any other objects appearing in awareness. And in Western gatherings you'll hear questions on what realization is like, how to gauge one's progress, the place of emotions such as jealousy and anger, free will versus determinism, realization and how to live life, knowing versus feeling, and how realization affects romantic, professional and family relationships.

All of these issues and questions are entry-ways into knowing your own nature and finding fulfillment.

What Is "Direct" About The Direct Path?

"Direct" is usually interpreted to mean "not progressive." In other words, you don't have to perfect anything or become anything new. You already are whatever you would seek to become.

Of course, this isn't different from many other types of nondual teaching. Most nondual teachings agree that "the seeker is the sought" and that there's no need and no possibility to become something else. But the Direct Path means something else by "direct" as well. "Direct" means "unmediated" and refers to the direct presence and clarity of your experience, which is not interpreted through intellectual or emotional filters. What seems to be a filtering or mediating process isn't that way at all. Instead, what seems to filter or operate on experience is actually already direct experience itself, direct experience masquerading as something else.

What is direct experience? Let's start with **indirect experience**. This is experience in which one thing is experienced by means of another thing. Examples would be experiencing Bali via reading the National Geographic, experiencing Las Vegas via seeing James Bond in **Diamonds are Forever**, experiencing fire through smoke, or experiencing an apple via our perceptions of it, such as taste, smell, texture, etc.

Direct experience, on the other hand, is the experience of something that is **not** interpreted or mediated by something else. In experiencing the "apple," we directly experience a red color, a crisp texture, a tangy flavor, etc. The experience of Bali is the same – what is given directly to experience is sensations, thoughts and feelings. We call them "Bali." The label is an interpretation. And yet we'll come to find out that direct experience is actually simpler than this. We discover that in direct experience there are actually no objects at all, and nothing pointing to any objects. This is beautifully simple. And just how we make this discovery is the purpose of this book.

All the various experiments, contemplations and visualizations that you'll encounter here are not ways to become awareness, or to gain an intellectual understanding that you are awareness. Rather, they are simply ways to explore the consequences of being awareness. You can think of these activities not so much as goal-oriented, but as exploration, celebration or beautiful music.

The Approach Taken Here

This book involves several different approaches.

- Standing as awareness, knowingly occupying and inhabiting your true identity, and experiencing the resulting confirmation of your stand.

- Simple remembrance that the body, mind and world are awareness as well. When we conceptualize them as independent objects, of course, they seem to come and go. And even then, if they come and go, the coming and going is taking place within awareness, which is the common factor. Body, mind and world are inseparable from awareness and are never experiences without awareness already being front and center in the picture. This can be experienced at any time if you just stop and try to find an object, any object that is apart from awareness.

- Abiding in the simple sweetness of being awareness, which is limit-less and borderless. This is also something that is available at any time if you stop and notice. The stopping and noticing, of course, won't be there all the time, but the beautiful truth they indicate is always the case.

- But mostly, this book will proceed as what Advaita-Vedanta calls "tattvopadesha."

Tattvopadesha is an experiential, logically-connected presentation of the teaching from beginning to end. It proceeds from the very concrete to the very subtle. It starts with the simplest and most seemingly obvious experience of separation, e.g., the experience of objects in the world that seem to be other than your self. You will see how these objects are nothing other than awareness. The tattvopadesha continues with more and more subtle elements of experience until we arrive at pure consciousness. Items we will examine include a vast range of experience, and we will proceed in order from the more concrete to the more abstract. You don't have to memorize this list and may not even need to explore everything on it. But the sorts of experiences we'll look into include the following:

- **Physical objects**, which are usually taken to be the textbook definition of reality.

- **The senses**, which are thought to be the neutral and transparent gateways to the world of physical reality.

- **The body**, including the brain, which is usually thought to be the container of the mind.

- **The mind**, which is usually thought to be the container of consciousness.

- **Events**, which are sort of like states of affairs, but with change and movement.

- **Mental states**, including emotional and meditative states, which all too often are experienced as more real than the ground we walk on.

- **Subtle abstract objects** such as cause and effect, identity and difference, time and space, subject and object. These subtle objects are often thought to provide a structure or organization to consciousness. We will see how consciousness cannot possibly be structured or organized by anything.

- **Witnessing awareness,** which starts out seeming like a big mind, complete with individuality, memory and psychological reactivity. But as our investigation continues, witnessing awareness comes to be understood as not possessing any personal, mental or psychological characteristics at all. Instead, it is realized that witnessing awareness is global clarity, and is what all characteristics appear to.

- **Pure consciousness,** which is consciousness without the witnessing aspect.

At each stage, we will have the chance to try experiments that make clear what we already know: what seems to be something other than awareness is awareness all the way and all the time. This is your happiness.

Separation – The False Claim Of Objectivity

Things seem to exist on their own, without depending on awareness in any way. Things seem to exist *objectively.* No matter how concrete or abstract something is, it seems to exist in this way. The Great Wall of China, differential calculus and moral correctness may not all be physical, but they seem to really exist independently from the mind and independently from awareness.

We think of the "objective" as that which exists on its own and which can be discovered and verified by separate "subjective" perceivers. The very notion of objectivity brings in several dualisms at once, such as between subjective and objective, between awareness and object, between separate containers of awareness, between inside and outside the container, and between "right" and "wrong" or "accurate" and "inaccurate." Many other dualisms also depend on the notion of objectivity.

Freedom From Objectivity AND Subjectivity

When we investigate objectivity and discover that it is not to be found, we do not fall into its opposite. We do not fall into subjectivity or solipsism. Instead, we become free from this pair of opposites. Nondual experience is neither objective nor subjective. Rather, what happens is freedom from the very structures that permit this distinction. We become free of its network of limiting assumptions, perceptions and feelings, along with the images of entrapment, containment and separation from people and objects.

Another dualism is the one between fact and value or intellect and emotion. The *first* member of each pair is usually accorded greater status than the *second* member, so the notion of objectivity often entails the dualism of ranking as well. When we try to "be objective" about something, we try to describe it as it is, impartially, grasped purely as it is in itself, without being swayed by emotion or evaluation. We feel we should see things from what is sometimes called the "View from Nowhere" or the "God's-eye View." Being able to perceive and judge this way is usually valued much more highly than letting any individual, personal, emotional or evaluative factors operate. The idea is that the object or situation pre-exists, and sentience or awareness is able to transparently and neutrally make contact with the object, thereby conveying true and accurate information about it. Any other way of grasping the object would be "subjective," which is usually de-valued.

When we feel that things exist objectively, it almost feels as if things are self-powered, persisting under their own steam. When we perceive things, it seems that things are casting themselves toward us, meeting our perception. There seems to be a kind of magnetism drawing our perceptual and conceptual energies toward things, which seem to be *really there*, but on the other side of a gap. Things seem to be on the far side of the gap, and we seem to be on the near side. Things seem to be "out there," and we seem to be "in here." To bridge the gap (which is usually thought to coincide with the surface of the skin), we must rely on perception and cognition. And we suspect that we can be wrong about things. We know that we must depend on perception and cognition, which can always be mistaken.

Because we seem to be "in here," we feel like we're enclosed in separate bubbles of sentience, one per person. So we also feel separated from other people. To bridge this gap, we need communication, which can also be mistaken.

The strong sense of these gaps causes great anxiety and suffering. The feeling that we are cut off, along with the ever-present possibility of being wrong about everything and everyone, creates alienation from the world, from other people and even from ourselves.

But our investigation will reveal in the most direct way that objectivity is false. We will see that no matter what kind of object is involved, *objectivity is simply never our experience.* The belief in objectivity and separation is simply unfounded. When this is deeply understood, partly due to the investigations we will undertake in this book, the misleading sense of objectivity will be understood as false and will eventually vanish. The entire structure that seems to keep us separate collapses, along with all suffering.

Without the sense of objectivity, there will be no sense of separation. All of the related dualisms and their attendant feelings of being split simply fall away. You will no longer seem to be separate from the world, other people or your own thoughts and feelings. You won't feel divided between thinking versus feeling. There will be no "out there" or "in here." You will not feel like a thinker or feeler or doer. You will realize your identity as the wholeness of all that is. This wholeness is experienced as love, peace and sweetness.

A Note About Terminology

Although some teachings distinguish awareness from consciousness, the Direct Path does not. In the Direct Path, the terms "awareness" and "consciousness" are synonyms. Neither one is more basic than the other, and there is nothing more basic or primordial that is "prior" to consciousness.[4] The term "awareness" tends to be used when objects are being discussed, and "consciousness" tends to be used when the collapse of the witness is discussed. But these are stylistic matters only. Either term could be used in either context.

And what *is* awareness? Descriptive terms can be philosophical or poetic, including: the ground of all being, THAT which everything is appeared to, the witness, the unseen seer, love, beauty, sweetness, being, clarity, reality, self-luminosity and peace.

Who Realizes? Who Is Writing This?

These questions sometimes come up at the beginning of inquiry, and a person wants clarity: "Who is the realizer? If it is **someone**, then is that truly a nondual realization? If it is **no one**, then what's the use and how does that benefit me? Who do you mean by 'I'? Who is writing this book? Is it being communicated from the absolute level or the relative level? If it is from the absolute level, then how can it say so many different things and actually recommend things to do? If it is from the relative level, then how do we know that what it says is true?"

Sometimes the nondual teacher's response to these sorts of questions mentions consciousness or no one. For example, these expressions are familiar, "It is consciousness talking to consciousness." Or "No one realizes that there is no one there."

I find that these can be helpful expressions in some cases. But in other cases, people can take them too literally. The listener can personify consciousness, thinking about it along the lines of a person who would be speaking or realizing. Or people can insert themselves into the term "no one." I had a friend who said, "You know, I want to be that 'no one' who realizes that there is no one there." In my friend's case, these expressions became retained and rehearsed as part of a new belief system that's given the label "nondual."

I talk more about language toward the end of the book, but here is a way to get started if these questions seem important. Feel free to begin this investigation without fixed answers to these questions. I am using the pronouns "you" and "I" in the everyday conversational sense, except where noted. You can begin by thinking of the realizer and the speaker the way you would normally think of these things if you were unacquainted with nondual theory. And then see what happens as you proceed. These issues will all receive intense scrutiny.

The only terms that I'm using in a special sense from the beginning are "awareness" and "consciousness." By these I mean "that to which appearances appear," or "the unseen seer." I don't use these terms to refer to a personally or biologically individuated sentience the way we would in the everyday sense.

If you do feel the "who realizes" question very strongly, you will probably feel its force diminish to zero as you go through the inquiry.

PART 1 – WORLD

*After we came out of the church, we stood talking for
some time together of Bishop Berkeley's ingenious
sophistry to prove the nonexistence of matter, and that
every thing in the universe is merely ideal. I observed,
that though we are satisfied his doctrine is not true,
it is impossible to refute it. I never shall forget the
alacrity with which Johnson answered, striking his
foot with mighty force against a large stone, till he
rebounded from it – "I refute it thus."*

James Boswell, **Life of Johnson**

*Through the senses, you perceive only gross objects. As
you transcend the first and reach the second stage, you
perceive only subtle objects or ideas. In the last stage,
everything appears as Consciousness.*

Notes on Spiritual Discourses of Shri Atmananda,
Vol. 2, p. 199, Note #1025.

The world is the collection of all objects. We feel that the world is *out
there* and that we are *in here*. This is our basic sense of separation.

What is an object? For many people, the textbook example of an
object would be something physical, such as a car, a tree or a rock. Feeling like we are inside a bag of skin looking out at objects is the paradigm
case of a sense of separation. We feel cut off from the world because of
this sense of separation.

In this chapter we will begin our examination of this sense of separation. We will begin to experience that the sense of separation is totally unsupported by our direct experience. When we realize that the sense of separation is not supported, we discover that it will not support suffering.

Physical Objects

When we hear someone say, "It is all the Self" or "Awareness is all there is," we immediately think of those rocks and trees. Maybe bridges, sky-scrapers and computers as well. How can these things be awareness? We often think of awareness as soft, penetrable and lighter than air. But physical objects seem to be hard, resistant, heavy and impenetrable – except with tools even harder than they are.

Rocks and the ground seem so different from awareness. If anything **isn't** awareness, these objects seem like the perfect candidates.

But what does our direct experience have to say about these things? We will investigate these things directly, and ask ourselves questions such as:

- Is awareness really something big and soft?

- Is a rock really something that possesses hardness within itself?

- Is a tree really something other than myself?

If something is really the case, then experience should be able to prove it. We will conduct experiments and investigations to discover what is proved by our direct experience.

Most of our suffering is based on the presumption that the mind, body and world are all separate and independent from each other, and independent from being seen, witnessed and known. We are fearful, shocked, indignant and even outraged if one of these aspects of reality changes suddenly or comes to an end. We take our self to be independent from everything else, and feel that this separate self should somehow be immune to change, poverty, shame, insults, disease, old age and death. We feel fear, sadness, depression, indignation and anger with the approach of any of these aspects. We want to be the separate enjoyer of everything, and we also want nothing to change. These desires are based on the presumption that things (including our own self) are objective. We feel that things exist independently, separately from awareness, and that they are really, truly *there*.

Our Strategy – Trying To Validate Objectivity

In order to tune in to our investigations, we will first examine the claims of objectivity and separation more closely. What exactly is being claimed? Then we will examine these supposedly separate objects in extreme close focus. We will investigate objects using the most direct and definitive evidence we have: our senses. We will examine the direct evidence proved by our senses, taking the senses individually, from easy to work with to more challenging. We will proceed in the order of Hearing, Seeing, Smelling, Tasting and Tasting.

The purpose of these experiments is this: by trying to validate objectivity, we will fail every time. We discover that we validate quite the opposite. We demonstrate experientially that what we *actually* experience is not objective, separate or alien, but actually limitlessness, inseparability and awareness.

So first, what is objectivity really saying?

Naïve Realism

> *Reality is that which, when you stop believing in it,*
> *doesn't go away.*
>
> Philip K. Dick

> *The primacy of existence (of reality) is the axiom*
> *that existence exists, i.e., that the universe exists*
> *independent of consciousness (of any consciousness),*
> *that things are what they are, that they possess a*
> *specific nature, an identity.*
>
> Ayn Rand, **The Metaphysical Versus the Man-Made**

In the West, however, the dominant notion of the real is largely based on disciplines such as physics and the psychology of perception. What is real, what really exists, is that which does not depend on the mind of the observer in order to exist. Reality is said to be mind-independent.

And, of course, physical objects seem to be the most obvious case of something real. The common-sense way we think about the world is that we perceive it directly. According to common sense, physical objects cause our perceptions of them. And on the other hand, our mental images resemble the physical objects. This is the view called "Naïve Realism," and can be depicted by the diagram below.

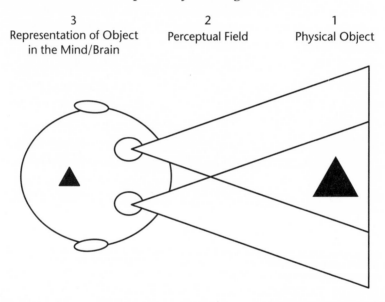

| 3 | 2 | 1 |
| Representation of Object in the Mind/Brain | Perceptual Field | Physical Object |

Figure 1 – Naïve Realism

You have probably seen variations of this diagram many times, even in school. It shows (1) the physical object, (2) the perceptual field and (3) the image of the object inside the head. Each component is separate from the others.

The important thing about this diagram is the claim of Naïve Realism: *the object exists regardless of whether anyone is seeing it*. The physical object does not depend on the perceptual field or the inner representation in order to exist. In fact, multiple observers are able to see the exact same object, because it exists before their observation and independently of their observation. This is what it is said to mean for the physical object to *exist* or *be real*.

After seeing so many of these diagrams, we come to take them literally. We may even think that there is a triangular image inside our head/brain/mind which resembles the external physical triangle that we think caused it. We think the same way about the other senses, with varying degrees of clarity and distinctness. For most people, however, vision tends to be the dominant sense and is the one they think *about* and think *with* the most.

But the remarkable thing about diagrams like this is that they don't correspond to anyone's actual observations. No scientist observes a triangular visual field surrounding a physical object, and then an identical mental object inside the head which matches the physical object. Regardless of the type of measuring equipment used, the scientific observer does not observe an image of the external triangle nestled among the neurons.

Not only does the external observer not see a scenario like Figure 1, but the subject doesn't experience anything like it either. When you are seeing an external physical triangle, you never observe your own "visual field" or rays of vision emanating from your eyes. You also never witness a mental object that you observe to match the physical object.

Diagrams like Figure 1 are simplistic conceptual constructions.

Naïve Realism is also vulnerable to another kind of difficulty which is called "perceptual relativity."

The Perceptual Relativity Critique

The appearance of the external object is vulnerable to a wide range of "objective conditions" such as distance, angle of approach, lighting, and the presence or absence of other objects in the vicinity. The more one thinks about how this happens, the more the question arises, "Why do we think that the object in itself is fixed and invariable, when our perceptions vary so widely?"

For example, let's say the object we are observing is a top of a burnished oak wood table in our living room. The table is said to be "round." That is, from an angle of vision centered directly above the table, the table top looks round. But when we enter the living room and look at the table, it seems flattened. When we approach the table and walk around it, the tabletop appears a little fuller than it did from the edge of the room, but certainly not round.

If the table is lying on its side, the ellipse is oriented a totally different way, now tall and thin rather than broad and flat.

In fact, the shape and proportions of the tabletop differ with almost every passing moment. We might never actually see the table from the angle in which it appears round. Yet we firmly believe that the table is actually round in and of itself, as though it has roundness **internal** to it as part of its nature.

And then there's color. When our grandparents gave us the table, they said it was "golden brown." Now it looks darker. It looks the most towards golden brown in the middle of a sunny day if we pull aside the curtains in the living room windows. At dusk it is grayish dark brown. And at night it appears a murky and blurry dark gray. Sometimes a dense black. Most of the time it does not appear to be brown. And let's say one evening we happen to be watching TV in the same room with our table. We see an advertisement from a furniture store for a brown table. The image will be intensely bright. The table depicted will have a brilliant, appealing golden brown color. Now we look at the physical table in our room, and it will look even darker and less brown than it looked before we saw the TV ad.

There are thousands of cases of perceptual relativity like these. We are so used to them that in order to maintain the belief in the constancy of the externally existent physical object, we have come up with a more complicated model than Naïve Realism gave us. This new model goes by many names, such as "Representative Realism" or "Indirect Realism" or "Common Sense Realism."

Representative Realism And The "Veil Of Perception"

Representative Realism tries to account for perceptual relativity by showing how the information coming from the external object is broken down and interpreted by the mind before the mental image arises. That is, the mind is said to play a more active role than it did in Naïve Realism.

In Representative Realism, perception happens in stages. The perceived object is still external, pre-existent and objective. But it sends us various signals, which we interpret so as to correctly and accurately re-constitute the object in our minds. Even intuition, the "sixth sense," can work this way. (In the West there are other more complex theories of realism as well. For the last several hundred years, realists have been arguing with idealists and nominalists and pragmatists and constructivists and, more recently, with postmodernists. A person can be a realist about one kind of thing, but not about another. But the various kinds of realism tend to agree that at least some things exist without depending on persons, minds, thoughts, languages, conventions or awareness.)

Representative Realism works like this. The object out in the world causes vibrations of different types. These vibrations are picked up by the senses and turn into sense data. The sense data are experienced as sensations and interpreted by the mind, after which the accurate mental image appears.

Representative Realism may be depicted in diagrams like this one:

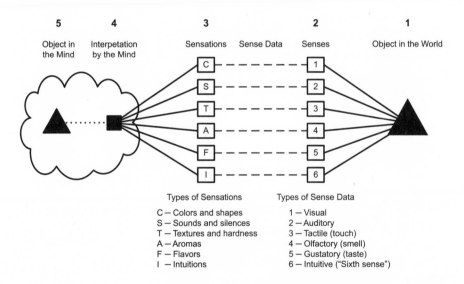

Figure 2 – Representative Realism

In Representative Realism, we do not experience the object directly, but through a veil of perception. There are actually several veils and gaps in the process, and each gap is designed to be able to account for perceptual problems. In addition to perceptual relativity, there are also other potential problems that the model needs to account for, such as illness when our senses (2) are not functioning normally. There are also possible emotional and psychological influences that affect the interpretive stage (4), such as being in love in such a way that every person on the street looks like our romantic partner, and cases of education and conditioning, where the object won't look like a table until we have come to learn what a table is. (Actually, all these situations are reasons **not** to accept Representative Realism, so the model must work harder!)

But in spite of all these stages, Representative Realism makes the same two claims that Naïve Realism makes:

- (C) The external object (1) causes the mental object (5).

- (R) The mental object (5) represents and resembles the external object (1).

And because of the two veils, the veil of the senses and the veil of mental interpretation, the idea of verifying claims (C) and (R) makes even less sense than it does with Naïve Realism.

But this intellectual conclusion is not enough to overpower the strong belief that there are thoughts and images "on the inside" and a world "on the outside" which match. We still think and feel as though there is a match in which the object causes the idea, and the idea resembles the object. We need to experience directly that this set of "realist" assumptions is never verified.

The Reality Effect

By "reality effect" I mean the feeling that something is really real, in the way described by some variation of realism. The reality effect is not the reality intended by the realist, but the conviction or feeling about such a reality. Certain experiences can convey a greater or lesser reality effect. Certain experiences can make us feel that something must be "really real." Certain experiences make us feel that there is something out there truly existing independently of thought and awareness.

For example, stubbing our toe in the dark has a greater reality effect most of the time than hearing a musical chime or seeing a pastel bedspread. The sense of touch usually has a greater reality effect than the sense of vision. Intense experiences have a stronger reality effect than mild experiences. Pain has a greater reality effect than pleasure. When people say, "Let's get real," they usually mean to accept something unwelcome.

We will look at the reality effect while examining different aspects of our experience. What is interesting is that the reality effect does not prove reality as the realist would wish. The reality effect is more like a combination of strong beliefs and feelings that make us convinced that reality is objective. This conviction could be described as follows:

(T) Mild experiences may well be illusory, but I feel that the intense or painful experiences actually point to objective reality.

(T1) The more intense the experiences, the more I believe that they point to objective reality.

Notice that both the reality effect (T) and the intensity with which it is believed (T1) are simply arisings in witnessing awareness. They are just like other thoughts. They appear in awareness and subside back into awareness. The reality effect is nothing more than that.

This brings us to our experiments.

Experiments

We will investigate our experience directly. We'll hunt for objectivity. We'll try to discover the actual presence of veils, levels and layers in our experience that would indicate that we are actually separate from objects and cut off from the world. In other words, we will try to verify whether (C) and (R) are true. Items (1) and (5) refer to parts of Figure 2 above. Item (1) refers to "objects in the world," and (5) refers to "objects in the mind." When we feel the Realist attitude, we feel that there is an interaction between (1) and (5). Usually we feel that:

- (C) The external object (1) causes the mental object (5).

- (R) The mental object (5) represents and resembles the external object (1).

Our inquiry will go like this. We will try to verify (C) and (R) by looking into reality and objectivity very carefully. If anything is objectively "out there" or "in here" as an independently existing thing, then it ought to be easier to find the closer we look. We will look very closely and directly. But we will not find anything separate or objective to actually exist. We will not find independence, division or separation. Instead, when we look very closely and directly, we will find wholeness, clarity, completeness and indivisibility. These are the legacies of our nature as awareness.

We'll proceed by experimenting with each sense separately. Later, we will experiment with combinations of senses in case there are any interaction effects which create a world through a process of senses working together.

The Source Of The Experiments

Where did these experiments come from? They actually have "street cred," because they are designed in response to many years of questions I've received from people actually doing nondual inquiry. The questions usually represent people's sticking points, places where inquiry has stalled for them. Some issues are more frequent than others, but each one turns up many times, according to my observations.

Each experiment is a potential way to see through one of these common issues. The issues all carry assumptions. The assumptions usually amount to regarding some aspect of experience as a truly existent object. What the experiments reveal is that all these objects have one thing in common. The objects cannot be found when looked for in direct experience. Only awareness is "found," and yet awareness is not an object. It is the very nature of experience itself.

Setup For The Experiments

While you do the sensory experiments and most of the other investigations in this book, do them with care. Find a quiet, peaceful place where you won't be in the way of anyone else. Some experiments might ask for the assistance of another person. Some of the experiments will require you to observe common objects such as a bell, a chair, an orange, etc.

To paraphrase the familiar product warnings, please don't do the experiments in this book while driving or operating machinery. These experiments can facilitate perceptual and gestalt shifts; you may experience feelings of disorientation at first. These experiments can upset the conventional ways you experience yourself and the world. Make sure to conduct the experiments in a safe place.

Before You Begin

Immediately before doing an experiment, take a few minutes to try what I call the "Heart Opener." It is akin to falling in love with awareness. It is akin to a reminder that awareness is the nature of you and all things. Experiencing this reminder opens the heart, and you'll find more ease and less resistance when doing the experiments themselves.

Being Awareness – The Heart Opener

1 Take a deep breath slowly. Exhale slowly, all the way. Take another deep breath. Exhale all the way. Now take three-quarters of a deep breath and exhale as you normally would.

2 Close your eyes. Notice that there might be sounds, sensations, feelings and thoughts arising, but that YOU, the witnessing awareness to which these things are arising, are always already present.

3 Notice that you are this clarity. You are present whether there are objects arising or not. **If there are objects**, you are already there as THAT which knows the **presence** of the objects. **If there are no objects**, you are already there as THAT which knows the absence of the objects. Regardless of the presence or absence of objects, you are there.

4 Notice that you are not an observed object at all, but the open, spacious, brilliant clarity in which objects arise. You cannot grasp or hold this clarity, for it is the very spaciousness in which grasping arises.

5 Notice that there are no walls to this clarity, no edges to YOU. You are borderless. You are not contained by anything. You are limitless.

This doesn't have to take long. You can do it just until you get a taste of yourself as this limitless awareness. There is a sweetness to this taste, which will cause you to fall in love with awareness all over again. And then when you do the experiments, it will guide you home.

Hearing

We will begin with hearing. For most people, hearing is not the dominant sense. For this very reason, it may be easier to work with, and the steps of the exercise can be understood more easily.

In the following exercise, we will investigate a *bell* through hearing. What direct evidence does hearing provide about the bell? We are focusing only on hearing, not on seeing or touching. Hearing is one source of direct experience and we will investigate it carefully. If any "evidence" seems to appear through other channels such as memory, thinking, feeling or touch, simply set it aside and return to hearing. Later, we will investigate the other channels directly as well.

Experiment 1 – Hearing The Bell

Purpose – Discovering what you really hear.

Objects needed – A bell or bowl of some kind. A wooden spoon or chopstick as a striker.

Setup – The bell can be a Zen-style temple bell, a gong or a single "jingle" bell. If none of these are around, you can use something from the kitchen, such as a metal serving tray, a mixing bowl or a coffee cup. For the striker, you can use a wooden chopstick or a spoon. If you can find a friend to strike the "bell" for you, this will make it easier for you to focus on **hearing** without moving your body or involving other senses. But you can do it by yourself if you cannot conveniently find someone to assist. The experiment can still work.

The Experiment – Begin with the Heart Opener so that you get a taste of being the open clear spaciousness of awareness.

1 Close your eyes. Have your assistant strike the bell (or if need be, do it yourself with your eyes closed). Let the sound subside.

2 Wait 5 seconds. Strike the bell again. Let the sound subside.

3 Repeat step (2) for a total of 3 strikes of the bell.

Inquiry – Inquire into what you have experienced directly. During the following inquiries, strike the bell again if you need to, in order to clarify and verify what you have experienced. Beginning with the experiment itself, whatever comes through hearing has been part of your direct experience. It may seem as though you "heard the bell." We will investigate it as it is done in the Direct Path. We are basically taking a very close and detailed look at what is directly experienced.

- **Do you experience a separate or independent perceiver?** One of the most common assumptions regarding perception is that there is an independent perceiver who is on the ultimate receiving end of incoming sense data. See item 5 in Figure 2 for a schematic image of this perceiver. But going by the sounds themselves and not by thought, inference or imagination, do you actually experience a separate hearer or perceiver? What would the hearer sound like?

- **Do you experience a bell to be independent of sound?** We usually think that the object (i.e., the bell) is a truly existing object which causes the impressions we have of it. This is the object that we think exists outside the "veil of perception." Let's see if this idea is verified in direct experience. *Don't go by what you think must be true in order to explain perception. Instead, go by your direct experience.* You do seem to experience the bell-sound. But *do you also experience a bell making the sound?* In other words, do you experience a **bell** in addition to the sound? If you do experience a bell making the sound, this would help verify the notion that the bell exists objectively. You would be directly experiencing an independent bell. You would be experiencing a bell existing outside your experience. But do you? Going by hearing alone, is there anything directly experienced about the bell other than a bell-sound?

▪ **Do you experience a sound to be independent of hearing?** We may think that not only the bell, **but the sounds themselves** are objective. This is because we think the objective bell is causing sounds to exist, which we then pick up and which becomes sensory information. We often think that the sounds are actually present, waiting for us to come along and hear them. But let's look into it more closely: *Do you experience a sound waiting to be heard, a sound outside the scope of your hearing*? In other words, do you directly experience a sound already present which you then proceed to hear? Yet another way of looking at this question would be: *Do you experience an unheard sound?* Also check: do you experience the sound as separate from you? Do you experience it to be at any distance from you?

▪ **Do you experience hearing to be independent of awareness?** We often think of hearing and seeing as actual objectively existing faculties or abilities. We consider them to be pre-existent tools that awareness makes use of. It seems that we can use these tools to pick up information about the "outside world." Let's look into that. *Do you experience hearing itself as something existing outside of witnessing awareness*? Do you experience hearing being already present in a pre-existent way, waiting to be taken up by awareness and used? Do you hear hearing? Now think about the other senses for a moment. Do you see hearing? Do you taste or smell hearing?

▪ **Witnessing awareness** – Try to scan your direct experience: *Do you directly experience a moment when awareness is absent*? Whether there are bell-sounds or not, do you experience a moment in which awareness is not there?

▪ **The claims of realism** – Remember the two claims of realism, (C) and (R)?

(C) The external object causes the mental object.
(R) The mental object represents and resembles the external object.

Did you directly experience anything that could support either claim? In order to substantiate claim (C), you would need to isolate and identify an external object. Then you would need to isolate and identify a mental object. And then you would need to trace a process between the external object and the mental object that proves that the first actually causes the second. This is the sort of thing that we do when we say that the soccer player's foot causes the ball to move. But in the case of a supposed external object and a supposed mental object, can you do this?

In order to substantiate claim (R), you would need to do something quite similar. You would need to isolate and identify both objects, and then stand aside from them and observe the resemblances between them. This is the sort of thing we do when we say that a portrait resembles a person. In the ideal situation, you can place them side by side and look back and forth between them, checking for similarities and differences. But in the case of a supposed external object and a supposed mental object, can you do this?

Review Of Hearing

Going just by hearing, and not by any other sense, and not by any theory about what must be true, what did you directly experience? Very likely you discovered something as follows:

The perceiver: No separate perceiver is given in direct experience.

The bell: There is no bell experienced to exist objectively outside the bell-sound. In direct experience, there is nothing more objective to the bell than sound. It's nothing more than sound (and as we will see, much less than sound). *No objective bell is experienced.*

The sound: And yet there is no sound experienced to exist objectively outside the hearing of the sound. There are no unheard sounds directly experienced. This is actually revolutionary. If there are no sounds experienced outside hearing, *then the idea that you heard a sound is not verified in direct experience.* To verify that you actually hear a sound, we would need independent access to the unheard sound. We would then need to show that this pre-existing unheard sound was then picked up by the faculty of hearing. But nothing like this scenario is given in direct experience. Going by your direct experience, what seemed to be sound is discovered to be just hearing. *No objective sound is experienced.*

Hearing: And yet even hearing is not experienced to exist objectively. There is no independent faculty of hearing experienced to exist outside of witnessing awareness. You don't experience anything like "non-witnessed hearing" that then becomes "witnessed hearing." *No objective hearing is experienced.*

Awareness: Awareness is "there" as presence. It's never absent. It's not an object that is able to come and go the way we think bells and sounds must come and go. Rather, awareness is that to which things appear. It is not present; instead, it is presence. And what appears, appears to awareness and only to awareness. In the case of the bell, the sound and hearing, awareness is the only common factor that is never absent. Regardless of what is found or noticed, and regardless of what seems to come up, awareness was always and already there. I hope that the heart-opening exercise helped make this experiential for you!

Realism: We know what would be required to support realism: we'd have to have access to external objects themselves, and then prove that mental objects match up to them or are caused by them. But we are never in such a position. So the realist claims (C) and (R) have not gained any support from our inquiries. We never find them supported in any way by direct experience. We tried our best to identify external objects and mental objects, and find relations of causality or resemblance between them. And we failed. We couldn't even isolate the objects in the first place. Therefore we could find no relationships between them.

The result is that realism and objectivity have taken a hit. The more deeply we realize this, the freer we become from separation. The wonderfully ironic thing about this freedom is that we don't have to stop talking about objects and perception and causality. We can use terms related to physical objects and causality to communicate with others, but we are free from taking them literally. We are free from feeling as though the referents of these words exist objectively and separately from us. We don't have to abandon our everyday lingua franca. But we no longer need to ***believe*** these words and concepts and feel separate because of them.

Seeing

> *Two painters were rivals in a contest. Each painter*
> *would try to make a picture that produced a more*
> *perfect illusion of the real world. One painter named*
> *Zeuxis painted a likeness of grapes so natural that*
> *birds flew down to peck at them. Then his opponent,*
> *Parrhasius, brought in his picture covered in a cloth.*
> *Reaching out to lift the curtain, Zeuxis was stunned to*
> *discover he had lost the contest. What had appeared to*
> *be a cloth was in reality his rival's painting.*
>
> A story from Ancient Greece

After investigating hearing, which is a simpler sense, we will investigate seeing, which is the dominant sense for most people. It seems much more complicated. We will follow with smelling, touching and tasting.

In the following exercise, we will investigate a simple orange through seeing. What direct evidence does seeing provide about the orange? While you do the experiment, focus only on seeing. If any "evidence" seems to appear through other channels such as touch, memory or thinking, simply set it aside and return to seeing. Later, we will investigate these other channels themselves.

Experiment 2 – Seeing The Orange

Purpose – Discovering what you really see.

Objects needed – A table or desk. A chair. A fresh orange. If finding an orange isn't convenient, then you can use an apple, an egg, a mouse from your PC. It will be helpful if the object you find has a uniform color and a smooth shape without too many sharp angles or corners. I will use the term "orange" in this experiment.

Setup – Find a fresh orange with a bright, uniform color. Clear a place on the table so that the orange can have 8-12" of clear space around it in every direction. Place the orange in the center of that space.

The Experiment – Sit in front of the table so that you are able to see the orange clearly. Rest your hands comfortably on your knees, palms up. This is to diminish any input from kinesthesia or the sense of touch. Begin with the Heart Opener so that you get a taste of being the open clear spaciousness of awareness.

1 Look at the orange and the table around it. If you see other details in the periphery, you can ignore them, as they are not needed for this exercise.

2 Focus on the orange for as long as you need to, until the table seems like part of the background.

3 Focus on the table, until the orange seems like part of the background.

4 Notice that if you go by direct visual evidence alone, the way you distinguish the orange from the table is simply by color. The orange is more or less a homogeneous expanse of the color orange. The table is a more or less homogeneous expanse of a different color, say brown or beige. According to your direct visual experience, the border *between* orange and table is an abrupt change in color.

5 Notice that according to your direct visual experience, no color is in front or in back of any other color. There might be a thought that says, "But the table is in back of the orange" – however, that is not direct visual evidence. You do not see one color behind another color.

6 Check for any shadow which may seem to be cast by the orange onto the table, or which may be visible towards the lower regions of the orange itself. In an everyday sense, a shadow implies depth. But going by direct visual experience alone, any "shadow" is merely a darker shade of color. It is either gray, a darker orange or a darker brown. There is nothing visible about the shadow other than a difference in color from the surrounding regions. What is true about shadow is also true about shine. It is a difference in color or intensity.

7   Check for small "indentations" in the orange. Normally, these would imply differences in texture, which imply differences in depth. But going by direct visual experience alone, they are merely small differences in color. They tend to be smaller differences in color than the difference between the orange and the table. But all these differences are directly experienced as simply differences of color.

8   Check whether you see any depth according to your direct visual experience. Do you actually see a third dimension? Color is two-dimensional. There is an orange shape, with brown above it, below it, to the left and to the right. There is no "close" or "far" or third dimension actually seen. This is how photography, cinema and trompe l'oeil painting work. Of course, a thought may arise, "Wait! The orange is closer to me than the table!" But the "closer" is not directly seen. What appears to be "orange closer to me" is experienced visually as an expanse of orange sitting "lower" in the visual field than the other expanse of color. "Higher up" in the display is assumed to be farther away in the world, but this depth or distance is an inference, not your direct visual experience.

Inquiry – As you ask yourself the following questions about your direct experience, you may look again at the orange as much as you need to.

• **Do you experience a separate or independent seer?** We are asking again what we asked in the hearing exercise. Do we directly experience the perceiver? Do we see that which is seeing? Is it our direct experience?

• **Do you experience an orange apart from the color?** We usually think that the color comes from the independent object and resembles the object. But do you actually see the object? Do you experience a physical orange existing behind the color or independent of the color? Do you experience an orange causing the orange color? Do you experience an orange that the color seems to be pointing to? Is there anything directly visually experienced about the orange other than color? **Do you directly experience an objectively existing orange? Does such a thing really make sense?**

▪ **Do you experience color to be independent of seeing?** Even though we do not experience an objectively existing orange, we may still think that the colors themselves are objective, existing out there waiting to be seen. But is this given in direct experience? Notice that we are not trying to assess the objective existence of a physical orange. We tried to do this in the previous question and came up empty. An objective orange was not established by direct experience. Here we are looking for something more subtle. We are testing to see whether even the colors exist objectively. To justify this claim of objectivity, we would need to experience the colors in some way *other than* vision and then verify that vision is successfully making contact with the same colors. This is sort of analogous to how detectives confirm an eye-witness report by checking other sources independent of that one report.

To do this visually, the only way to verify the independent existence of a color is to visually experience a color that is present but unseen and to then verify that vision actually sees that same color. In other words, we would have to use direct experience to compare an unseen color with a seen color. *But do you directly experience an unseen color?* What does it mean for a color to be present but unseen? Where is it while it is unseen? Does an unseen color make any sense? And if an unseen color doesn't make any sense, then how can a seen color make any sense?

Also check: do you experience color as separate from you? Do you experience it to be at any distance from you?

▪ **Do you experience shape to be independent of color?** Going by direct visual experience, do you experience color without shape or shape without color? The orange is round. But do you ever visually experience an orange color without some kind of shape, or a shape without some kind of color?

▪ **Do you experience seeing to be independent of awareness?** We often think of seeing as an activity or a faculty or a set of physical organs that exist independently of awareness. We can now ask whether seeing is directly experienced as such. *Do you experience seeing as something existing outside of witnessing awareness*? Do you experience seeing being already present in a pre-existent way, waiting to be taken up by awareness and used? If it seems that you do experience seeing to exist in this objective way, how is it experienced? *Do you actually see seeing? Do you hear it*? Is there any way that you directly experience the sensory modality known as "seeing" to be outside of awareness or independent of awareness? It turns out that "seeing" is nothing more than awareness itself.

▪ **Witnessing awareness** – Try to scan your direct experience: *do you directly experience a moment when awareness is absent*? Whether color seems to be there or not, do you experience awareness to come and go? Do you experience a moment in which awareness is not there?

▪ **The claims of realism** – Remember the two claims of realism, (C) and (R)?

(C) The external object causes the mental object.
(R) The mental object represents and resembles the external object.

Did you directly experience anything that could support either claim? These claims describe clearly how we think perception is. We think that our perceptions are caused by external objects. We also think our perceptions represent and resemble external objects. This splits the world of experience dualistically into two: (1) **outer** objects that we think cause **inner** objects, and (2) **inner** objects that we think look like **outer** objects. In my own life, this kind of dualistic assumption always felt very alienating and made me feel separate and very alone.

But if you can't validate the claims (C) and (R), then you become free of them. The way we do this in nondual inquiry is to try to validate them and experience the utter failure of our efforts. This frees us of the power that the assumptions (C) and (R) have over us. Specifically, the way you would validate these claims would be to successfully identify an external object, then a mental object. For (C), you would then need to find a causal relationship between the two objects. And for (R), you would need to find a resemblance or other representative relationship between the objects. If you cannot find the objects, and if you can't find the relationships, then you are free from believing that the world is like this.

Review Of Seeing

Going just by seeing, what did you directly experience? Very likely you discovered something like the following:

The perceiver: No separate perceiver is given in direct experience.

The orange: In this experiment, there is no orange experienced to exist objectively outside the orange color. In direct experience, the color is all there is to the orange. It's nothing more than color. *No objective orange is experienced.*

The color: And yet there is no color experienced to exist objectively outside the seeing of the color. There are no unseen colors directly experienced. There are no colors experienced to be hanging out in the shadows, waiting to be seen. As in our hearing experiment, this is revolutionary. If there are no colors experienced outside seeing, *then the idea that you see a color is not verified in direct experience.* Color is not independent of shape, so neither of them can exist objectively and independently. You are not able to attain non-visual access to color in order to verify that vision actually contacts a pre-existing color and gets it right. Going by your direct experience, color and seeing pretty much amount to the same thing. *No objective color is experienced.*

Seeing: And yet even seeing is not experienced to exist objectively. Wherever there is seeing there is witnessing awareness. There is no independent faculty of seeing experienced to exist outside of witnessing awareness. You don't experience anything like "non-witnessed seeing" that then becomes "witnessed seeing." *No objective seeing is experienced.*

Awareness: Awareness is "there" as presence. It's never absent. It's not an object or a thing that is able to come and go the way we think oranges and colors must come and go. Rather, awareness is that to which things appear. It is the subject to which arising objects appear. In our experiments, awareness is the only common factor that is never absent.

Realism: Again, our two realist claims (C) "the external object causes the mental object" and (R) "the mental object represents the external object" were not supported in any way by direct experience. Realism and objectivity have taken another hit, this time from the results of an experiment with our dominant sense. What's more, these results can be replicated and verified at any time.

According to your direct experience, the only "reality" is the intimate presence of awareness itself, not an objective world.

Smelling

The next sense we'll explore will be smelling – olfaction. It is considered to be a relatively simple sense but also "primal." This means that olfaction arrived early in evolutionary biological history and that it's deeply embedded in experience. Examples of the embeddedness of the sense of smell are familiar. You've probably heard how slight whiffs of long-forgotten fragrances can bring up distant but intense memories and associations. Other senses don't have this capacity in such a pronounced way. We won't be looking into this particular aspect of olfaction right here, because we'll explore memory and association on their own later when we investigate the mind.

What we will investigate is the same thing we searched for with hearing and seeing: *does direct experience verify the seeming independence of the object?* When smelling happens, it normally seems as if there is an independent object that is smelled. It really seems as though the very process of smelling establishes this. Our investigation will look deeply into this seemingness – is it our direct experience that a separate, independent object is there?

In our exercise, we will use our orange again. We'll focus only on smelling. If any "evidence" seems to appear through other channels such as memory, thought or bodily sensations, we'll set it aside and attend just to our direct experience coming through the sense of smell. We will investigate attention and the other channels of experience later.

Experiment 3 – Smelling The Orange

Purpose – Discovering what you really smell.

Objects needed – A table or desk. A chair. A fresh orange. A knife. A pile of books. A plate and a napkin. If possible, a partner.

Setup – Find a fresh orange or use the same orange you had used in Experiment 2 (Seeing). Cut the orange in half. Fold the napkin and place it on the plate. (The napkin will help prevent the orange from rolling around.) Place the orange onto the napkin, flat-side up. You will be smelling the freshly cut flat surface of the orange. *If you find that you are unable to smell the orange, then substitute another fruit such as a lemon, peach, apple, strawberry, banana, etc.*

This exercise is best done by focusing on the sense of smell with a minimum of interference from other senses. For example, if the plate is too low on the table, you may end up leaning your body towards the plate. You may inadvertently associate the sensations of leaning with the fragrance of the orange, whereas they are actually two independent sense experiences. For this reason, the optimal case would be to sit comfortably in a chair with your eyes closed, and have the orange positioned exactly underneath your nose! You can do this easily if another person is available to help by holding the plate. If not, then you can use a pile of books underneath the plate to boost the orange up to nose-level.

The Experiment – Sit in front of the table, in front of the orange. Rest your hands on your knees comfortably, palms up. Begin with the Heart Opener so that you get the bloom of the heart-opening clear spaciousness of awareness.

1 With your eyes closed, smell the orange. Once the fragrance is noticeable, continue to experience it for a period of up to 15 seconds.

2 For a period of about 15 seconds, take a short olfactory break. Turn your head away from the orange. Since your eyes are closed, this is only an approximate guess. It can also be accomplished by indicating to your partner to pull the plate away for 15 seconds.

3 Repeat steps (1) and (2) for a total of five times.

4 Notice that the fragrance of the orange seems to be present and a bit later seems not to be present. Or at least it may seem to be stronger and then weaker.

5 Going just by smell and not by imagination, visualization or any bodily sensation, check whether you directly experience "depth" or "distance." These attributes are usually interpreted as degrees of separation between the perceiver and an independent, external object.

Inquiry – As you ask yourself the following questions about your direct experience, you may smell the orange as much as you need to.

- **Do you experience a separate "smeller"?** We normally believe that perception, in this case smelling, is done by a separate person, sense organ, faculty or sense modality. But do we actually experience this directly? Check very closely. Somewhere in or around the fragrance of orange, do you directly experience the fragrance of a smeller? Let's say that you seem to smell a bit of Old Spice or Chanel No. 5 mixed in with the orange. This is not direct experience of an independent smeller. It is merely a discernibly different fragrance. And the same inquiry needs to take place about *that* fragrance as about the orange!

- **Do you experience an orange to be independent of fragrance?** We usually think that the fragrance is caused by the independent object, and that the fragrance must be an indicator of that object. So now, going by olfaction alone, do you directly experience an orange independently of the fragrance? Do you directly experience a causal process in which an independent physical orange is "out there" manufacturing a fragrance and transmitting it to you? **Do you directly experience an objectively existing orange?**

- **Do you experience fragrance to be independent of smelling?**

It can seem as though the fragrance is out there just waiting to be intercepted by the sense of smell. But this is a thought-based conclusion. In this experiment we are sticking to the direct evidence of smell itself. So we must ask whether we directly experience a fragrance to exist apart from smelling. But such independence is not experienced even in dream or imagination. Wherever there is fragrance, there is smell. The other senses are exactly parallel to this.

To test for the contrary, you would need to somehow encounter fragrance other than through smelling, and match that up to what you smell, assuring yourself that they are the same thing. In other words, you would have to somehow smell an unsmelled smell and compare it to a smelled smell. The very requirements of such a test are ridiculous and incoherent. And yet this is what would be required to directly experience a fragrance that is truly objective and independent. Our direct experience is never incoherent. What's incoherent is the body of assumptions that say that things exist separate from experience.

Also check: do you experience the fragrance as separate from you? Do you experience it to be at any distance from you?

▪ **Do you experience smelling to be independent of awareness?** Like hearing and seeing, we may also think of smelling as something that exists independently of awareness. But is that our experience? Ask yourself, *"Do I experience smelling as something existing outside of witnessing awareness?"* Do you experience smelling being already present in a pre-existent way, waiting to be taken up by awareness and used? *Do you actually smell smelling?* And even then, what makes it independent of awareness? Do you ever catch it existing outside of awareness?

▪ **Witnessing awareness** – Try to scan your direct experience: *do you directly experience a moment when awareness is absent?* Whether fragrance seems to be there or not, do you experience awareness to come and go? Do you experience a moment in which awareness is not there?

▪ **The claims of realism** – Remember the two claims of realism, (C) and (R)?

(C) The external object causes the mental object.

(R) The mental object represents and resembles the external object.

Did you directly experience anything that could support either claim?

Review Of Smelling

Going just by smelling, what did you directly experience? Very likely you discovered something like the following:

The perceiver: No separate perceiver is given in direct experience.

The orange: In this experiment, there is no orange experienced to exist objectively outside the orange fragrance. In direct experience, the smell is all there is to the orange. It's nothing more than fragrance. *No objective orange is experienced.*

The fragrance: And yet there is no fragrance experienced to exist objectively outside the smelling of the fragrance. There are no unsmelled fragrances directly experienced. There are no fragrances experienced to be hanging out in space, waiting to be smelled. This is radical. If there are no fragrances experienced outside smelling, then the idea that you smell a fragrance is not verified in direct experience. You are not able to attain non-olfactory access to fragrance in order to verify that olfaction actually targets a pre-existing fragrance and gets it right. Going by your direct experience, fragrance and smell pretty much amount to the same thing. *No objective fragrance is experienced.*

Smelling: And even olfaction is not experienced to exist objectively. Wherever there is olfaction there is witnessing awareness. There is no independent faculty of smelling experienced to exist outside of witnessing awareness. You don't experience anything like "non-witnessed smelling" that then becomes "witnessed smelling." *No objective smelling is experienced.*

Awareness: Awareness is "there" as presence. It's never absent. It's not an object or a thing that is able to come and go the way we think oranges and fragrances must come and go. Rather, awareness is that to which things appear. It is the subject to which arising objects appear. In our experiments, awareness is the only common factor that is never absent.

Realism: Again, our two realist claims (C) "the external object causes the mental object" and (R) "the mental object represents the external object" were not supported in any way by direct experience. Realism and objectivity have taken another hit, this time from the results of an experiment with a very primal sense. What's more, these results can be replicated and verified at any time.

The only "reality" is the intimate presence of awareness itself, not an objective world.

Touching

The sense of touch may be the most important sense for our inquiry into the assumed objectivity of the world. It is a very authoritative and complicated sense.

The sense of touch is **authoritative**. It has perhaps the greatest reality effect of all the senses. This is because in case of conflicts, the sense of touch is granted the right to contradict or prevail over the other senses. For example, if you walk into another room and suddenly SLAM into something, you will investigate. "Aha," you will say. "That was a glass door!" It was squeaky clean and you didn't see it. You may then conclude that vision was "wrong" in that case and that bodily contact (the sense of touch) was right. Speaking in "realist" terms, if the world seems to be one way as indicated by vision, and another way as indicated by touch, we more often go with touch.

We seem certain that touch conveys the way objects are in themselves.

Of course, most of the time, we strongly feel as though touch and vision work together to establish the objective world. We feel pretty sure that things are "out there" in the world in a pre-existent way. We feel as though the tactile and visual senses pick up vibrations caused by these pre-existing things, and that we touch the very same things that we see. This interactivity between senses seems like "double proof" of an objective world. Sensory interactivity, especially between vision and touch, deserves special investigation. We will cover it toward the end of this section.

The authority of the tactile sense also comes up when people think of objections to nondual teachings. Where a teaching might say that everything is awareness, a frequent objection is that I might be hit by a car. This is essentially why Johnson kicked the rock when he was discussing George Berkeley's immaterialist philosophy. He thought that his kick was a successful refutation. Johnson's response is certainly clever in a poetic way! And even today, it is considered added proof that the world of touch disproves the world of awareness.

But there is a shocking secret – if we investigate directly, the world of touch isn't experienced as disproof of awareness at all. Quite the contrary! The sense of touch sweetly verifies that your direct experience, the very "world" itself, is nothing but awareness.

The sense of touch is also **complicated**. An entire book on nondualism could be written on the sense of touch. The sense of touch involves many different kinds of experiences that are associated with the skin, body or world, including:

- **Texture** – The feelings of rough and smooth, wet and dry, soft and hard.

- **Temperature** – The feelings of warm and cool.

- **Extension** – The feelings of area, breadth and height (the two-dimensional "spread-outness").

- **Pain** – The feelings of being pressed upon, cut, punctured, hit, etc.

- **Position** – The feelings of the hand or other parts of the body being in a certain posture, configuration or location. This is basically the sense of proprioception.

- **Movement** – The feelings of the hand or other parts of the body moving with respect to other parts, or moving together with respect to the world. This is basically the sense of kinesthesia.

- **Various ideas** – Thoughts of existence, reality, distance, surface, volume, size, depth, resistance and blockage, such as "my hand is touching this," "this object is [x] far from me," "there is a surface here," "this must be real."

But in this section, which focuses on whether the sense of touch proves the objectivity of the world, we will concentrate on the types of sensations that are unique to touch, which are **texture** (including roughness/smoothness, wetness/dryness and hardness/softness), **temperature** and **extension. Pain, position** and **movement** will be covered when we investigate the body. The various **ideas** associated with touch will be investigated when we cover the mind.

The strategy of our experiments. We are breaking the sense of touch into various components. We will directly experience each component by itself and see that it never proves objectivity or separation from awareness. If no single sensation is able to establish separation from awareness, then neither can the sensations establish separation when they are experienced in combination. Of course, the reality effect of combined sensations is more powerful than the effect of any sensation by itself. But the reality effect is itself merely another experience and never points beyond itself to any object separate from awareness.

We will experience directly that the sense of touch, just like hearing, seeing and smelling, proves nothing other than awareness!

Experiment 4 – Touching The Table

Purpose – Discovering what you really touch.

Objects needed – A table or desk. A chair.

Setup – In this experiment you will be sitting at the table touching its surface. You'll be going just by the sense of touch, concentrating on various elements of roughness/smoothness, wetness/dryness, softness/hardness, temperature and extension. You'll be investigating whether there is objectivity of any kind given in direct experience.

You will do the experiment once for touch in general. After that you will be doing the experiment again, focusing on each of the various categories of touch: roughness/smoothness, wetness/dryness, temperature, hardness/softness, extension.

The Experiment – Sit in front of the table. Rest your dominant hand above the table so that it is not touching anything. This is the hand you will use in the experiment. Rest your other hand comfortably on your lap, palm up. As always, begin with the Heart Opener.

1 With your eyes closed, allow the dominant hand to touch the surface of the table. Once the texture is noticeable, continue to experience it for a period of at least 15 seconds.

2 Raise your hand from the table for a period of about 15 seconds. The sensations might seem much more subtle now, or it might seem that no sensations are occurring. In either case it is a change, and either case is OK.

3 Repeat steps (1) and (2) for a total of five times.

4 Going just by touch and not by imagination, visualization or any other sense, check whether you directly experience something objective, external or pre-existing that is being touched by you. Is an external physical object given in direct experience?

Inquiry – As you ask yourself the following general questions about your direct experience of touch, you may touch the surface of the table as much as you need to.

▪ **Do you experience a separate "toucher"?** We normally believe that perception, in this case touching, is done by a separate person, sense organ, faculty or sense modality. But do we actually experience this directly? Check very closely. Somewhere in or around the texture of the surface of the table, do you directly experience the sensation of a toucher? Let's say that you seem to touch a bit of a grainy pattern. Is this direct experience of an independent toucher? Or is it merely a texture?

▪ **Do you experience a table to be independent of texture?** We usually think that the texture is an inherent characteristic of the independent object, provided by that object. So now, going by the tactile sense alone, do you directly experience a table or the surface of a table independently of the texture? Do you directly experience a causal process in which an independent physical surface of the table is "out there" manufacturing a texture and transmitting it to you? **Do you directly experience an objectively existing table?**

▪ **Do you experience texture to be independent of touching?** It can seem as though the texture is out there just waiting to be intercepted by the sense of touch. But this is a thought-based conclusion, not given in the direct experience of touch. In this experiment we are sticking to the direct evidence of touch itself. So we must ask whether we directly experience a texture to exist apart from touching. But actually, such independence is not experienced even in dream or imagination. Wherever there is texture, there is touch.

Experiment 4a – Touch And Roughness/Smoothness

Repeat steps 1-4, this time focusing on just the sensations of roughness and smoothness. Add these considerations to your inquiry: What is given in your direct experience? Is there graininess, sharpness, dullness, a lined or ribbed texture? Do you experience a cause of the texture? Do you experience an experiencer of the texture? Do you experience a texture apart from touch? Do you experience touch apart from texture? Do you experience touch apart from witnessing awareness?

Experiment 4b – Touch And Wetness/Dryness

Repeat steps 1-4, this time focusing on just the sensations of wetness and dryness. Add these considerations to your inquiry: What is given in your direct experience? It there a damp, wet or moist sensation? Or a dry, scratchy sensation? Do you experience a cause of the dryness, such as something causing a lack of moisture? Do you experience an experiencer of the wetness or dryness? Do you experience wetness or dryness apart from touch? Do you experience touch apart from some degree of wetness or dryness? Do you experience touch apart from witnessing awareness?

Experiment 4c – Touch And Temperature

Repeat steps 1-4, this time focusing on just the sensations of warmth and coolness. Add these considerations to your inquiry: What is given in your direct experience? Is there a sensation of warmth or coolness or an indeterminate neutrality? Do you experience a cause of the warmth or coolness, something creating just that degree of warmth or coolness? Do you feel an independent object that is warm or cool? That is, do you feel something behind the warmth or coolness that happens to have these properties? Or is it just a sensation of warmth or coolness? Do you experience an experiencer of the warmth or coolness? Do you experience warmth or coolness existing apart from touch? Do you experience touch apart from witnessing awareness?

Experiment 4d – Touch And Hardness/Softness

Repeat steps 1-4, this time focusing on just the sensations of hardness and softness. The sensation of hardness or softness has a powerful reality effect, and can make us feel that there is something independent from our experience that is actually "there" as an objectively real, pre-existing object. Notice that the experiences of independent existence and objectivity are conclusions that arise in thought. They are not given in the direct experience of hardness itself. Also, the sensation of hardness can make us feel as though we are being resisted, rebuffed or rejected. These experiences arise in thought, and they can also be emotional reactions that rise in relation to memories, wishes, fears and hopes. The feeling of being resisted or rejected is not something given directly by the sense of touch. We will examine emotions, conclusions and thoughts later when we investigate the mind. For now, if these experiences arise, simply return to the direct experience of hardness or softness that is given in touch.

Add these considerations to your inquiry: What is given in your direct experience? Is there a sensation of some degree of hardness or softness? Do you experience a cause of the hardness? Do you experience an experiencer of the hardness? Do you directly experience a hardness that exists apart from touch? Do you experience touch apart from some degree of hardness or softness? Do you experience touch apart from witnessing awareness?

Experiment 4e – Touch And Extension

Repeat steps 1-4, this time focusing on just the sensations of hardness and softness. The sense of extension is the sense of spread-outness, of a continuity going left/right and up/down. Like the sensation of hardness, the feeling of extension also has a fairly convincing reality effect. In fact, some Western philosophers have believed extension to be one of the defining characteristics of physical objectivity and reality. This is exactly what we will investigate. Does the experience of extension, of a continuity of sensation of left/right and up/down prove that something is independent from awareness? Do you experience "continuity," "left and right" or "up and down" as independent from awareness? Or are they concepts (thoughts) only? Do these considerations demonstrate anything other than awareness? Or do they demonstrate awareness only?

Movement and extension. Of course, you can have a stronger feeling of extension if you move your hand left/right, up/down or in a circle. But in this case, some of your experiential cues are coming from the feelings of kinesthetic movement, that is, the feelings of moving your arm and hand. Combined with these sensations are the thoughts that claim that "I am moving my arm, an independent physical object, against the table, another independent physical object." Of course, this is a very convincing thought. But it is only a thought and not the direct experience of objectivity or independence of an object. For this reason, try to focus on the sensation of extension without moving. If this is not possible, then try moving your fingers or wrist as gently as possible. *Try to be focused on just the feeling of extension,* not the kinesthetic sensation of movement or the claims made by thought. We will investigate movement and thought later.

Add these considerations to your inquiry into the sense of extension: What is given in your direct experience? In addition to the sensation of extension, do you directly experience an object that is extended? Does the experience of extension by itself prove the existence of an independent table? Does the experience of extension prove an object that exists apart from experience? Notice that if there is an experience of the "table," the "table" experience is a thought or visualization or memory.

Inquire also into these issues: Do you experience a cause of the extension? Do you experience an experiencer of the extension? Do you directly experience an extension or surface or substance that exists apart from touch? Do you experience touch apart from witnessing awareness?

Review Of Touching

Going just by touch, what did you directly experience? Very likely you discovered something like the following:

The perceiver: No separate perceiver is given in the direct experience of touch.

The table: In this experiment, there is simply no table experienced to exist objectively outside the various textures, coolnesses, hardnesses and feelings of extension. In direct experience, the touch is all there is to the table. It's nothing more than the direct experience of touch. *No objective table is experienced.*

The texture/smoothness/dryness/coolness/hardness/extension: And yet there is no texture or smoothness or dryness or coolness or hardness or extension ever experienced to exist separately from touch. No untouched textures are directly experienced. Neither is there any untouched hardness or smoothness or extension. There are no textures or any of these other objects experienced to be pre-existing in space, waiting to be touched. None of these arise in direct experience. These things are not like what we normally think of as untouched textured objects like nail files or pieces of sandpaper. In everyday language it makes sense to speak of a nail file that I am not touching now. But this is the radical discovery: it makes absolutely no sense to speak of an untouched texture (or hardness or coolness or dryness).

If there are no textures experienced outside touching, then the idea that you touch a texture is not verified in direct experience. You are not able to attain non-touched access to any of these qualities in order to verify that the tactile sense actually comes into contact with them. Going by your direct experience, doesn't it seem that the arising of these qualities and the sense of touch amount to pretty much the same thing? *No separate quality or object is experienced.*

Touching: And even the tactile sense is not experienced to exist objectively. Wherever there is the tactile sense there is witnessing awareness. There is no independent faculty of touching experienced to exist outside of witnessing awareness. You don't experience anything like "non-witnessed touching" that then becomes "witnessed touching." *No objective touching is experienced.*

Awareness: Awareness is "there" as presence. It's never absent. It's not an object or a thing that is able to come and go the way we think tables and textures must come and go. Rather, awareness is that to which things appear. It is the subject to which arising objects appear. In our experiments, awareness is the only common factor that is never absent.

Realism: Again, even against the sense of touch, which has such a strong reality effect, our two realist claims (C) "the external object causes the mental object" and (R) "the mental object represents the external object" are not supported in any way by direct experience. Realism and objectivity have taken another hit, this time from touch, which is usually their strongest ally!

The only "reality" is the intimate presence of awareness itself, not an objective world.

To Do On Your Own

If you wish, perform these same experiments with the orange. Instead of touching the surface of the table, touch the flat surface of the orange which you had exposed by cutting the orange in half. This will provide a set of sensations much different from the table-sensations.

Tasting

We have saved the sense of taste for last. Although the sense of taste is not dominant or authoritative like vision or touch, it is quite complicated. It is like touch in having the aspects of texture, roughness/smoothness, wetness/dryness, coolness/warmth, hardness/softness, extension and movement. But in this exercise we will concentrate on what is unique to taste – the *flavor* aspect. We will investigate whether there is any separation or objectivity in the direct experience of flavor. Does flavor prove any object separate from awareness?

The sense of taste often dovetails with the sense of smell. When we experience and categorize the world in terms of external physical objects, we think that things taste and smell "the same." It often seems that the two senses reinforce each other. But not always. The durian fruit (*Durio zibethinus*) is an exception, great teaching opportunity. It helps debunk the opinion that the sense of smell and the sense of taste are two effects of the exact same causes. Durians upset this expectation: even though they smell like sewage, they taste like delicious vanilla custard! Perfumes are exceptions too. They can smell like chocolate, strawberry or vanilla. But they taste bitter and acidic. Although we think of the senses as being inter-related because of being effects of the same external objects, we will come to experience that not only are there no objects to be found, but that the senses are quite independent arisings, with no causality operating in any direction.

Experiment 5 – Tasting The Orange

We will concentrate on the "flavor" element in the sense of taste. We will taste a slice of an orange. If the orange from previous experiments is still available, you can use it.

Purpose – Discovering what you really taste.

Objects needed – A table and chair. An orange. A knife. A plate.

Setup – Find a fresh orange. Cut five or six bite-size slices and place them on the plate in front of you.

The Experiment – Sit in front of the plate. Begin with the Heart Opener so that you can establish the open clear spaciousness of awareness.

1 Take a bite of one of the orange slices. Close your eyes.

2 Begin to chew the slice of orange until the flavor emerges. Stop for about 30 seconds.

3 Focus on just the flavor (and not on the texture, coolness, wetness, etc.). The flavor might include sweetness, bitterness, tartness, sourness and tanginess.

4 Finish chewing, swallow and wait for about 30 seconds. Open your eyes.

5 Repeat steps (1)-(4) for a total of five rounds.

Inquiry – As you ask yourself the following questions about your direct experience, you may take another bite of orange as needed!

▪ **Do you experience a separate or independent taster?** Again, this is the inquiry into who or what is tasting. Keeping just to the sense of flavor, do you experience a perceiver? That is, do you taste a perceiver? Of course, there might be thoughts that say, "There must be a separate perceiver if there is a separate orange slice." But those are just thoughts, and we will scrutinize the direct experience of thought at a later stage. Right now we are inquiring into just what is given in the direct experience of taste. Do you taste that which is tasting, something similar to what is depicted in **Figure 2**? Is it your direct experience?

▪ **Do you experience an orange to be independent of flavor?** For your experience to certify the independent existence of a physical orange, you would have to experience the orange in an independent way, in some way that would not depend on flavor. In this experiment, yes, you do seem to experience flavor. But besides flavor, does your direct experience actually include the separate existence of a physical object, the orange? One way to check for a physical object being experienced apart from the flavor would be to ask this: in addition to the flavor, do you experience a *cause* of the flavor? If so, what does the cause actually taste like? What is it in this direct experience that makes it a cause, as opposed to merely an aspect of flavor itself? Does flavor give you the direct experience of its own cause?

▪ **Do you experience flavor to be independent of tasting?** The same question we asked about an orange independent of the flavor can be asked about the flavor itself. Do you directly experience flavor apart from the sense of taste? For our experience to certify the independent existence of something, it must be able to be experienced independently. Is the flavor able to be experienced independently of the sense of taste? Is your experience providing another way to experience the flavor, somehow not depending on taste? That is, **do you directly experience an untasted flavor?**

▪ **Do you experience tasting to be independent of awareness?** We are now asking the same question about tasting that we just asked about flavor. *Do you experience tasting as something existing outside of witnessing awareness?* Do you experience tasting being already present in a pre-existent way, waiting to be apprehended taken up by awareness? Do you ever taste anything if witnessing awareness is not already present?

▪ **Witnessing awareness** – And now we ask the same sort of question about witnessing awareness itself. Is there ever a moment when you experience witnessing awareness to be absent? If so, what is it like?

Review Of Tasting

Going just by tasting, what did you directly experience? Very likely you discovered something like the following:

The perceiver: No separate perceiver is given in direct experience.

The orange: In this experiment, there is no orange experienced to exist objectively apart from flavor. In direct experience, the flavor is all there is to the orange. It's nothing more than flavor. *No objective orange is experienced.*

The flavor: And yet there is no flavor experienced to exist objectively outside the sense of taste. There are no untasted flavors directly experienced. If there are no flavors experienced outside tasting, *then the idea* *that you even taste a flavor is not verified in direct experience.* Flavor is not independent of the sense of taste: to experience flavor is itself the arising of the sense of taste. *No objective flavor is experienced.*

Tasting: And yet even the sense of taste is not experienced to exist objectively. Wherever there is taste, there is witnessing awareness. There is no independent sense of taste experienced to exist outside of witnessing awareness. *No objective tasting is experienced.*

Awareness: Awareness is also not experienced to exist objectively or apart from you. It never comes and goes. It's never absent. Things seem to come and go in awareness, but awareness never seems to come and go. In our experiments, awareness is the only common factor that is never absent.

Realism: Again, our two realist claims (C) "the external object causes the mental object" and (R) "the mental object represents the external object" were not supported by our experiments in tasting. Realism and objectivity have taken another hit. What's more, our results can be replicated at any time.

According to your direct experience, the only "reality" is the intimate presence of awareness itself, not anything sensed.

Intensity

Intensity adds to the reality effect. As experiences gain in intensity, they seem to gain in credibility as well. An intense experience seems as though it points reliably to something true. A mild experience doesn't seem as real. It seems as though we can write it off as imagination or illusion.

This is why intense sensory experiences such as vivid colors, loud noises or intense pain seem to signal objective reality. It seems like they **mean business!**

But if you look into the reality effect of intensity, it isn't substantiated in any way.

Start with a mild experience, like a slight tickle. An example might be a faint sound, like the traffic hiss you hear outdoors. It may seem unreal, not indicative of anything objectively the case. OK, now gradually add intensity, which in this case would be volume or even discomfort. For example, think of a very loud crashing noise sounding like it's coming from another room. It's a surprising noise – it's loud and maybe even "hurts the ears." The mere addition of this intensity seems to add a reality effect. Now that the sound is intense, it seems like it is really coming from a place outside perception, whereas the faint sound probably doesn't have this effect. The faint sound is almost able to be passed off as imagination.

So as these noises gain in intensity, do they actually become real? Do they actually signify a truly and objectively real cause, a cause that operates from a point outside of awareness and which has an effect of the sound inside awareness? What does intensity have to do with "reality"? And where does the cut-over happen from **not-real** to **real**? Say, between 0% and 100% on one's personal meter of intensity, does reality start at 67%? 99%? Where does "reality" begin?

Not only that, but after our explorations in sensing, just what would objective existence be? We gave objective existence a very good chance. We looked with great care. But we saw that when it comes to "objective" physical objects existing independently and apart from awareness, we didn't find anything but awareness itself. We never found independence or objectivity to be our experience.

Intensity seems to signal reality. But this is simply a thought, perhaps like the following:

(T2) Mild sensations are illusory, but intense sensations point to objective reality.

The thought (T2) is merely itself an arising in witnessing awareness. And the *strength of belief* in (T2) is merely another thought, such as (T3):

(T3) Hmm, it seems that (T2) is true.

Like the other thoughts (T) and (T1) we considered a few pages above (in The Reality Effect section), both (T2) and (T3) are mere thoughts that arise and subside in witnessing awareness. The reality effect of intensity is nothing more than that.

Movement

The common sense view of the world is that our bodies are physical objects in a world of other physical objects. And physical objects can move. In fact, Western philosophy has long held movement to be one of the defining qualities of physicality. Rocks and trees and wheels and persons can move. But ideas and purposes and propositions can't move. White objects can move, but whiteness itself can't move.

We can look at movement in terms of the sensory experiments we recently conducted, because the movement we are examining here is the movement of (what normally seem to be) external objects. There is another kind of movement, locomotion, which we'll cover later. Locomotion is more complicated, because in addition to experiencing the sensations of moving colors or changing sounds, we also seem to be purposefully moving the body "from the inside." We will explore this below when we explore the body.

- **Hearing:** When sounds change in pitch or volume, it seems more convincing that we are hearing an external, independent physical object. It might even seem to be moving towards us.

  But in direct auditory experience, we have discovered that there is never any concrete evidence of an object or sound existing apart from hearing. So it is not our direct experience that we ever "hear a sound." Sure, this arises as a way to speak, and this is fine. "I hear a barking dog over there." But when investigated closely and directly, it is not strictly accurate. There is no independent dog directly experienced. There is no barking that is experienced as existing waiting to be heard. There isn't even a directly experienced "over there" in hearing either.

  So if there is no direct experience of an independent, separate **object** apart from hearing, then adding the notion of **movement** cannot create objectivity. Through a change in pitch or volume, nothing objective can come into experience that was not present already. Movement is supposed to be the change in spatial position of something that was already present, but stationary. And this is exactly the point. We never directly experienced any object that was already present. In the very same way, we do not ever directly experience an object that is present but moving. We can speak of movement, which is a perfectly fine way for language to take place. But we do not need to believe and feel the separateness of objects that are assumed to exist separate from each other and separate from ourselves as awareness.

▪ **Seeing:** Seeing is parallel to hearing in this way. When the colors seem to change, we sometimes conclude that something is flickering on and off, or that something is moving. It's not that we think that colors themselves move. It's more that we think that color change is a sign of an external independent object that is moving. And when a color patch grows in size, we think that an object is getting closer in space. We may even experience an expectation that the sense of touch will soon kick in.

But in direct visual experience, we discovered that there is never any concrete evidence of an object or color existing apart from seeing. It is not our direct experience that we ever see a color, much less a pre-existing external object. We speak as though we actually do see these things. But upon examination, this has not been substantiated. We can regard talk of movement as convenient short-hand to summarize certain kinds of experiences, but we are free from having to take this talk literally.

This insight can be solidified. If we experience no independent object that is *stationary*, how can we all of a sudden experience an independent object that is *moving*? What does a change in direct experience have to do with whether an object exists apart from that experience? A change in color seems like a more complex experience than an experience where color does not seem to change. But mere change cannot create independent existence and separateness where none was experienced to exist without change.

And as we will come to see, the very notion of "change" depends on conceptualization and memory, which, when examined directly, never establish what they seem to point to. Change and memory never point to any external objects or object not present. They always point directly to awareness. We will cover these issues when we investigate the mind in Part 3.

▪ **Smelling:** The realization with the sense of smell is also parallel to what we realized with hearing and seeing. With the sense of smell, when the fragrances or odors change in intensity or other qualities, it seems that an object is moving closer to us or farther from us. This is parallel to sound, where we realized that sounds do not establish independent objects that cause the sound, or which sound represents.

▪ **Touching:** When textures or degrees of hardness or temperature change, we are trained to conclude "movement." The sense of touch is extremely convincing when it comes to concluding the existence of external objects.

Much of the persuasiveness of touch comes from its association with fear and the possibility of pain and damage. We feel, "How could my hand get cut unless my body is one physical object and the knife is another physical object which acted upon my body in space?" We will investigate pain and damage to the body in the next section on Body. But the direct experiences of texture, temperature, hardness and wetness themselves do not establish the existence of any independent object, even when the experience seems to be that these qualities are changing.

Even though the sense of touch is very persuasive, when it comes to the sense of an independent external world of objects, we have seen via careful investigation that separateness and objectivity are still not established through direct experience. There is no independent object or texture or hardness actually experienced as present to be touched. The realization with the sense of touch is parallel to the other senses. Adding *change* to the experience does not establish the independence of a causal or external object.

▪ **Tasting:** The sense of taste is quite similar to the sense of touch, but with the added element of flavor. Change in flavor can seem to mean that an object in your mouth is shrinking, becoming softer or getting old. But there was never any object or mouth directly experienced in the first place. So the seeming change in experience cannot establish objectivity that was not experienced in the absence of change.

Review Of Movement

In all these cases, the notion that an object is moving is a belief based on a sense that a sensation is changing. This change in sensation is a sort of flow, something other than inactivity. But in all our investigations so far, we have not yet directly experienced any objects as present and independent from sensation or awareness. This means that we haven't directly experienced any *stationary objects or any moving objects*. The sort of flow experience is itself something that is not experienced apart from seeing, hearing, touching, smelling or tasting, even in imagination. So even though this sort of experience seems to be arising (we will consider later whether it really does arise), we have no experience of a flowing, changing or moving object.

To Do On Your Own

If you wish, you can invent and conduct your own experiments with what seem to be moving objects. Sit on the front porch and watch people and cars go by. Watch the TV screen. What makes you think an array of colors is actually something with independence and three-dimensional depth? Listen to various noises at home: heaters, air conditioners, refrigerator sounds, the purring of a cat, creaks in the building. Touch various surfaces, dragging your fingertips across textures and shapes. Kick (gently!) a couch or table leg. Notice that these things can be spoken of as though they are independently real objects and events and actions. But it is just language. There is no necessity at all to take any of it literally. There is actually a great degree of sweet, spacious freedom in this, in not demanding that the world match up in its nature to how you happen to speak so as to guarantee a literal point-to-point correspondence. See if you can get a taste of this freedom. And in this sweetness, try the experiments. Is there some kind of objectivity or independence from awareness that you discover that the experiments fail to account for? If so, look at it as directly as you can and see what happens!

Subtle Reality Effect – Agreement Between The Senses?

I seem to be able to see and touch the very same cup. This is something that seems to be an exception to the investigation we performed so carefully about the senses. One can understand how our direct experience is only awareness when we look at the senses *one by one*. That's how we do that investigation. We ignore any input from other senses.

But what about when we **don't** ignore the input from the other senses? That is, what about when the senses interact? Do seeing and touching actually point to the very same external thing? It seems like the investigation up to this point can't account for this interaction, and that there might be true objectivity and separation after all. The nondualist might just be imagining things or doing wishful thinking!

It is something that I puzzled about for many months back in my George Berkeley seminar in graduate school. And it is a question I get several times a year from people who are doing intense direct-path-style inquiry.

Here's how it works, and why the reality effect seems so strong.

I seem to see a cup on my desk. I seem to touch the same cup. There arises a very strong sense that the cup, the very same cup, exists apart from me. In fact, it seems more convincing than if I had seen the cup without touching it, or touched the cup without seeing it. It seems like the cup is existing somehow between the senses. Of course, this makes for a much more powerful reality effect. Since "cupness" seems to be coming through multiple senses, I can feel like I dare not ignore the possibility that the cup truly exists independent of observation. It seems like it's really and truly **there**. This added certainty is like when many witnesses agree on who robbed a bank.

Earlier, we used an orange for many of our experiments. When the senses interact, it seems that we are one physical object perceiving another physical object through multiple channels. We may imagine the schematic process to be as follows:

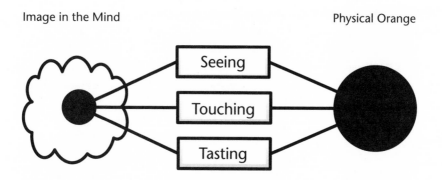

Figure 3 – Sensory Interaction

We imagine one external cause (the orange), its properties being communicated to us through a variety of sensory corridors. So it seems that we are getting a reinforced message of the orange's existence and independence. It seems like excellent, almost irrefutable evidence that the orange is really *out there,* and that we are really *in here* (in the mind).

Common Sensibles – The Perceptual Source Of Objectivity?

The root of this feeling of sensory reinforcement is the notion of certain core qualities sometimes known as "common sensibles." I'll explain more about them below, but first, some examples:

- The orange looks round and feels round.

- A pair of dice looks like it's really two objects and feels like two objects.

- One of the pair – it looks cubical and feels cubical.

- A corner looks angular and feels angular.

- A tabletop looks flat and feels flat.

In general, roundness, squareness and flatness are sometimes said to be "common sensibles," that is, qualities available to more than one sense.

Not all qualities are like this. Some qualities, such as color, taste, odor, warmth and coolness, seem more tied to a single sense and more "subjective" or dependent upon the observer. We learn to associate one sense to another by long practice. So we associate red with hot and blue with cool. We become able to discern visually what kind of surface is wet to the touch. We become able to tell by touch just how tight to tune the drumhead for a crisp sound. But since these associations are not 100%, we can easily be mistaken about these things. For example, we can be fooled by something looking wet and touch it, only to learn that it is a trompe l'oeil or "hyper-realistic" painting on the sidewalk.

But certain characteristics, including size, shape, position, motion and rest, have been thought by certain realist philosophers to be able to convey the *same* information through *multiple* senses. These qualities have been thought to be independent of any observer, and therefore true qualities of physical objects. These qualities are said to be "common sensibles." This is why we feel so sure about the roundness of the orange and the squareness of the cube.

Of course, the more certain we feel about the objective shape of the orange, the more we feel that we, too, are a physical object that perceives it. This model of objective existence, with its internal and external aspects, is the basis for a deep sense of separation, with its attendant suffering.

But as we shall see, our direct experience does not verify this in any way. Our direct experience of the perceptual situation is nothing but global awareness. There are two ways to see this.

Falsifying Interaction – Two Ways

We can become free in two ways from the added reality effect caused by sensory interaction.

One way is through nondual investigation that examines *thought* in addition to sensation. The other way is through the insights of the "Molyneux Problem." Thought is also a component of the interaction between senses. We will examine thought closely in a later section (Part 3), but here is a capsule summary of how thought gets involved. When we seem to see and feel the roundness of an orange, our experience is as follows:

1 A visual sensation arises.

2 A tactile sensation arises.

3 A thought arises, claiming that (1) and (2) point to the same thing: roundness.

Thoughts like (3) make a claim about something "objective" that is supposed to truly be the case. But there is never any experiential confirmation of this claim. Sensation cannot confirm anything. As we have seen in our experiments with the senses, no sense by itself can possibly substantiate a claim made about anything objective, since sensations themselves don't "point" to anything other than awareness. They *are* awareness. So adding two sensations together cannot provide any additional confirmation of a claim made by thought. Zero + zero = zero. So you will see that the supposed objectivity is nothing more than a claim made by thought.

And even that little scenario is too complicated. It is only provisional. This is because after we see in the next section that the body is not a physical object but only awareness, and that there is no experiential distinction between "inside" and "outside," we will deeply realize that there is no experiential distinction between thoughts and sensations. So-called "objects" will be experienced as nothing other than arisings in witnessing awareness. This is the "higher" or non-phenomenal witness which is equivalent to liberation since there is no entity of any kind left. And sometime after that, you will experience the dissolution or collapse of the distinction between arisings and awareness, which leaves you and the world as nothing other than pure consciousness.

The other way we can become free of this reality effect doesn't even require that we "go nondual." Science itself has provided a gripping puzzle about sensory interaction whose results dovetail nicely with those of nondual inquiry. The puzzle comes from a letter written by William Molyneux in 1688.

The Molyneux Problem And The Reality Effect

> *A Man, being born blind, and having a Globe and a*
> *Cube, nigh of the same bignes[s], Committed into his*
> *Hands, and being taught or Told, which is Called the*
> *Globe, and which the Cube, so as easily to distinguish*
> *them by his Touch or Feeling: Then both being taken*
> *from Him, and Laid on a Table, Let us suppose his*
> *Sight Restored to Him; Whether he Could, by his Sight,*
> *and before he touch them, know which is the Globe*
> *and which the Cube? Or Whether he Could know by*
> *his Sight, before he stretch'd out his Hand, whether he*
> *Could not Reach them, tho they were Removed 20 or*
> *1000 feet from him?*

Letter from William Molyneux to John Locke,
July 7, 1688

With this letter to John Locke in 1688 began one of the most fascinating puzzles about perception in the history of Western science. William Molyneux was a scientist and politician in Dublin who was interested in questions about perception. The puzzle he set forth came to be known as the "Molyneux Problem."

In more modern terms, Molyneux was posing this problem:

1 A man is born blind, but can distinguish the difference between a sphere and a cube by touch.

2 He regains his sight.

3 Can he now distinguish the sphere from the cube by sight, without touching them?

This problem is a challenge to believers in "common sensibles." Usually, believers will answer, "Yes." This is because it seems to them that if touch and vision actually convey information about the objective properties of roundness and squareness (or sphericity and cubicity), then the shapes are there right in front of the Molyneux man's eyes as soon as he is able to see.

There was a great deal of philosophical speculation answering on both sides. But what was the empirical, scientific answer?

Empirical Results

In 1728 a London surgeon by the name of William Cheselden was able to provide the first empirical answer to the Molyneux Problem. Dr. Cheselden published an account in which a boy born blind with cataracts was able to have them removed, thus allowing him to see.

When the boy was first able to see, he couldn't make out the shape of anything at all through vision alone. He was unable to perceive size or shape, and could not distinguish and name anything corresponding to his well-trained sense of touch.

Since Dr. Cheselden's results, there have been many other experiments bearing on this question. Although pre- and post-operative conditions have differed greatly, the results have never strongly supported the idea that untrained vision would confirm what is communicated through touch.

Of course, *trained* vision can associate back and forth with touch. Visual sensation can be associated through habit and training with taste, touch, sound, etc. This kind of association between senses is what happens even between sensations that are *not* the so-called "common sensibles," such as wetness, shape, size, number and location. It turns out that so-called common sensibles work the same way. Associations come to be formed through naming and labeling.

For example, a bark, a furry texture, a moist feeling, a visual image and a series of marks on paper such as **d o g** are all given the same verbal name or sound-label ["dawg"]. Many different sensations are conveniently treated as one thing. This does not establish that there is actually one single fixed, objective, pre-existing, independent thing, external to all observers, which serves as a single cause of all these sensory arisings. There is simply no empirical evidence in the Molyneux case for this contention.

In other words, a multi-sensory object, whether it is supposed to be an orange or a Rubik's Cube, is not really *discovered*, but *constructed*, including the qualities of "roundness," "squareness" or other "shape" characteristics. We think certain qualities like roundness or squareness are apprehensible by two senses. The "roundness," we think, is the very same thing, accessed in two different ways: through vision and touch. That is what we think. But what IS "roundness"? It is a conceptual, abstract object.

In terms of direct experience, the blind man in Molyneux's experiment first touches something and apprehends changes in texture and resistance. Some aspects (the ones that get called "air") are very non-resistant. Other parts (the ones that get called "sphere") are resistant. Then, with the benefits of teaching and communication, the Molyneux man infers roundness from what he senses. So far, this process is based on textures and resistance through touch. Later he is able to see. After some time, training and practice, colors are added to his repertory. He learns to associate certain color changes with certain texture changes and calls them "roundness" or "squareness."

But a texture is not a color. In direct experience these two sensations have nothing in common between them other than a thought or conclusion that makes a claim.

"Shape" is an abstract idea that we put together, imagining that there's something objective out there that textures and colors both point to. But the objective existence of shape is impossible even in theory to verify. The very idea of "shape" may even create a feeling of separation! In my own case it certainly did, and reinforced the entire sense of a "world out there" and a "me in here." But in direct experience there is simply no "common sensible" (where "common" means "common to more than one sense.") Even objectivity and separation, as we will come to see, seem to exist only because thought claims so.

The World – Conclusion

We have now examined the set of physical objects commonly known as the "world." We looked very closely at the best evidence – direct experience – for the possible existence of the world of concrete, independent physical objects. And we discovered something astounding in every case. We discovered that the only "thing" verified was awareness itself. We verified awareness and always failed to verify the many objects that are supposed to exist outside of the realm of awareness. Direct experience also failed to verify the independent existence of the senses as faculties or abilities. In every case we were led back to awareness that was the only constant factor in experience. We discovered that all there is to an orange, a bell or a table is awareness.

At this point it is common to think, "Ah, but perhaps we are limited by our senses and intellectual abilities. Maybe there really is something out there, but our tests are unable to find it." This is basically the idea that there may be stuff outside of awareness that is beyond our reach at the present. We will go deeply into this suspicion and the thinking behind it when we examine the "container metaphor" in Part 2.

PART 2 – BODY

The nurse comes in and says, "Doctor, there's an invisible man here for an appointment." The doctor says, "Tell him I can't see him."

Overheard in a doctor's office

The body seems to be part of the world. But it also seems to be that which perceives and feels the world. And it seems to be where we are localized.

The way we normally think of the body, it seems to be a physical object. But unlike a table or car, the body seems to be endowed with sentience. The body can perceive. It can feel pleasure and pain. The body contains the mind – and some people would say that there is no "mind" strictly speaking, but that it's the **brain** which is programmed to do everything that is called thinking. The body seems to be the locus of a vast function of consciousness. The body seems to be where "I" am localized. We think, "Maybe rocks and trees are able to see and feel too, but my own body and the ability to see and feel all seem bundled up into one. This body certainly seems to be where I am!" It seems as though I come and go with the body. And it seems that I began when the body began, and that I will cease when the body ceases.

In this part we'll explore the body. This is of paramount importance in one's investigation into one's nature. In many nondual teachings, the body gets left out. For various reasons, most of the attention goes to feelings and thoughts. But if the body is not explored in a direct way, then there will still remain a sense of localization and identity that seems rooted in the body. If the body is ignored, it will not be experienced as awareness, but rather as an unacknowledged container of awareness. Or simply a blind spot. This can create a sense of separation or alienation, as though the body were some sort of exception to the nondual investigation that examines other things. Even the thoughts and feelings that are examined and loosened up in nondual teachings can carry a subtle quality where they seem to be arising "here," which translates into a spatial designation. And, of course, if there's a "here," then there is also a "not here," which is a very sticky dualism.

When we investigate the body, we will see in different ways that the body is nothing but the lightness and sweetness of awareness itself. Whether experience seems to be orgasmic pleasure or intense pain, direct experience discovers nothing to the body other than the clarity and freedom of awareness. The body is not the container or conduit for awareness. The body doesn't perceive awareness. The body just is awareness.

We will explore the body in three ways, and in each of these ways, we will discover that our direct experience is that the body is nothing other than awareness.

As An Object

First, we'll investigate the body as another case of a physical object, just as we investigated the world. We will discover that the body doesn't sense, but arises as sensations, the same way a table or an orange does. We have already seen how these "sensations" are nothing other than witnessing awareness.

As A Feeler

Next, we'll investigate the body as something that seems to feel. It seems to feel when objects (including the body itself) touch it. We will investigate pains, pleasures, itches, twitches, movements and the sense of the body being located in a place. We'll discover that in direct experience there is no evidence that these experiences are felt **by a body or in a body**. We'll discover that these experiences, as well as the body itself, are nothing other than witnessing awareness.

As A Container Of Awareness

Finally, we'll investigate the sense that the body contains awareness. This includes the sense that there seems to be an inside and an outside to the body, and we seem to be on the inside. It also includes the sense that awareness seems to be inside the body and that I feel a limitation, because awareness seems to be global, yet I have no access to another person's thoughts. It seems that other people are separate containers, apart from *this* one. This is a very common perplexity, for students at all levels. We will discover that in direct experience there is no basis for the dualism of internal/external and the notion of containment. The question about "another's thoughts" is realized as a question that makes assumptions about awareness that have no basis in your own direct, limitless experience. Awareness isn't "physical" like a bubble. You will discover that the sense of inside/outside is never experienced to correspond to any objective fact. Based on your direct experience, you discover that the very senses of "place" and "enclosure" dissolve into openness and clarity·

The Body As Object

Let's look at the body as if from the "outside." There is a way that we experience the body the way we experience a table or chair, or as we experience another body. We see our arms, legs, hands, feet or torso. In a mirror, we can see what really seems to be "our" face, head and neck. With the aid of photography we can see what seems to be the back of our head.

We can touch most parts of our body. When we touch our body, it's very different from touching a table or chair. The experience of touching the body seems to be split into two parts, the part that does the touching and the part that is touched. In the case of the hand touching the elbow or the head, the "touching" part is the hand's sense of the hardness of the elbow or the hairiness of the back of the head. The "touched" part is the elbow or head's sensation that something touched it.

In this section we will cover the "touching" part of the body-object, which is the experience of touching an object that happens to be the body. This is part of how the body arises as sensations, because we touch and see and smell and taste this object as we do other objects.

In the next section we will cover the "touched" part of the body.

The body as feeler includes the experience of being touched. We'll also examine the various sensations of senses of itches and tickles, as well as the feelings of pain and pleasure, kinesthesia and proprioception.

We will discover in every case that the body is nothing other than witnessing awareness! Now that we are more familiar with the world-as-sense and ultimately as awareness, we will be able to examine the body-as-sensed, taking the senses individually. We will proceed in a more familiar order with the senses: seeing, touching, hearing, smelling and tasting.

Seeing The Body

The body arises to vision as colors.

- In "seeing your hand," colors arise and get distinguished from other colors called "background." The same process happens with seeing your feet or legs or knees or arms. One part of the color array is picked out and given the label, "me" or "my hand."

- "Seeing yourself in the mirror" or in a photograph is more indirect. The process also consists in the arising of certain colors along with a designation claiming that some of them are your body. But it is also indirect because the image in the mirror or the photograph seems like it is "not really me, but an image of me." It doesn't seem like my body began when the image began, and if the image ceases to exist, my body will probably still be here.

Is it really my body that I am seeing? What makes this color a part of me, and another color part of the background? We will explore this in the following experiments.

Experiment 6 – Seeing The Body

Purpose – Discovering how the body is experienced to arise in vision.

Objects needed – A table and chair.

Setup – Sit quietly in front of the table.

The Experiment – Begin with the Heart Opener so that you can establish yourself as the open clear spaciousness of awareness. Place your hands comfortably on the table.

1 Look at your hands for a period of 5 seconds.

2 Look off to the side for 5 seconds.

3 Close your eyes for 5 seconds. Open your eyes.

4 Repeat steps (1) – (3) for a total of five times.

Inquiry – As you ask yourself the following questions about your direct experience, feel free to revisit any of the steps above.

■ In step (1), keeping only to direct experience of seeing (and setting aside thinking, memory, imagination, etc.), is there any direct experience of a hand **causing** a color that arises? In other words, it may seem as if you are seeing your hand, but in the direct experience of **vision alone**, is there any evidence that the colors that arise are being caused by a hand?

■ In step (1), is there any direct experience of a color arising apart from vision? Do vision and color ever arise independently of each other? If not, that is, if color and vision always arise together, then how can it be that you actually "see a color"? You never experience a color that is there, unseen, waiting to be seen by vision. This is like an implosion, a radical experience that color is never experienced to be an independent object. The same lack of independence follows for vision itself. Do you ever experience vision in the absence of witnessing awareness? Is vision something that you experience to be present, which is then picked up by witnessing awareness to be apprehended? If not, then what do you ever experience other than the presence of witnessing awareness?

■ In step (2) (where you are looking away), is there any direct experience of a hand missing? The colors in step (2) are different from the colors in step (1). But is there any direct experience in step (2) of the lack of a hand?

- In step (3) (where your eyes are closed), are there any colors arising to vision? Is there any color that is still present? Is there any color that is experienced as absent or missing? Is there any visual experience of a body?

- To summarize: when colors are appearing, is there any direct visual experience of a body present that is causing the colors? And if colors are not appearing, is there any direct visual experience of a body that is either present or absent?

To Do On Your Own

Perform the same experiment with other parts of the "body" known as arms, hips, legs or feet.

Perform the experiment while looking in the mirror or at a photograph or video of "yourself." Notice how strong the sense is that the image (which we have learned in the "World" section is nothing more than colors) is your body or **represents** your body.

What makes those colors your body? Does your body come and go with the coming and going of those particular colors? Do *you* come and go with those colors?

Touching The Body

This experiential module is about touching the body. **Touching** the body is more complicated than **seeing** the body, because there are several possibilities. When you see the body, there is only **one** set of sensations arising. But when you touch the body, there often seem to be **two** sets of sensations that arise. Let's say you touch your knee. There will be (i) the sensation that we say arises "from the hand," and (ii) the sensation that we say arises "from the knee." There will be feeling that we designate as coming from both the "toucher" and the "touched." We imagine there to be two separate channels of communications bringing in the experiential data.

It seems like two separate channels because we really believe that the body is an independent physical object with different parts that are endowed with sentience. And in the case of the body touching itself, we think that data is being collected from two separate physical locations and transmitted through different sensory corridors. When this data reaches the mind, we believe, it gets interpreted correctly as the independently existent sentient body touching itself.

This experiment will investigate whether there is any direct evidence to support these beliefs. We learned in the section on the "World" that the sense of touch never provides direct experience of an object separate from awareness. In fact, the sense of touch confirms awareness only. We will discover the same thing in our direct experience of touching the body, even with this extra seeming complication. It is all the same: awareness is all that will be confirmed.

Experiment 7 – Touching The Body

Purpose – Discovering how the body is experienced to arise in touch.

Objects needed – A chair.

Setup – Sit quietly in the chair.

The Experiment – Begin with the Heart Opener so that you can establish yourself as the open clear spaciousness of awareness. Close your eyes.

1 Touch your knee. That is, allow your hand to rest lightly on the knee for 5 seconds. You can move your hand back and forth if this helps make the feeling more noticeable.

2 Remove your hand from your knee for 5 seconds.

3 Repeat steps (1) and (2) for a total of 3 times. Open your eyes.

Inquiry – Remember the supposed two sources of feeling when the body is touched? We will account for them in our inquiry. You may or may not be able to distinguish the feeling of "touching" from the feeling of "being touched." That is, the experience may just feel like one undifferentiated feeling of touch. Or it may allow you to distinguish the feelings into "touching" and "being touched."

Either case is fine. There are no wrong answers in direct experience! We will inquire into the experiment in both ways. In Case A, we will proceed as if we can distinguish the "toucher" and the "touched." In Case B, we will proceed as if it is one experience that can't be differentiated.

CASE A: Two separable experiences: touching and being touched

For most people most of the time, the experience of touching the knee can probably be differentiated into the experience of touching and the experience of being touched. So let's first examine the part associated with the experience of touching the body.

Touching

- In step (1) above (where you touch the knee), sensations arise: texture, warmth, a certain degree of hardness/softness, etc. Among these sensations, is there any direct experience of a knee being touched? Is there any direct experience of any physical object at all that is independent, pre-existent and letting itself be perceived through touch?

- Keeping just to these sensations, is there any direct experience of the sensations being felt by a hand? Does the hand arise in this direct experience?

- In steps (1) and (2), is there ever any direct experience of a sensation or an object that is missing? If it seems to be so, then just what does a missing sensation feel like? Just what is missing? And how does a sensation indicate this?

- In step (1), is there any direct experience of a texture arising apart from the sense of touch? Does texture ever arise independently of the sense of touch? If not, that is, if the sense of touch always arises when texture arises, then how can it be that you really "feel a texture"?

You never experience a texture that is there, untouched, waiting to be perceived by the sense of touch. This is a radical pointer to how texture is never experienced to be an independent object. The same follows for the sense of touch itself. Do you ever experience touch in the absence of witnessing awareness? Is touch something that you experience to be present, which is then picked up by witnessing awareness to be apprehended? If not, then what do you ever experience other than the presence of witnessing awareness?

- In steps (1) and (2), is there any direct experience that sensations arise in the absence of witnessing awareness? Is witnessing awareness ever experienced as being absent?

Being Touched

- In step (1), where it feels like your knee is being touched, what arises in direct experience? A sensation arises of a tickle, or degree of hardness/softness, maybe a sense of warmth or coolness. Does anything else arise to the sense of touch? Keeping to the sensations that arise (as we would normally say) "through the knee," is there any direct experience *that a hand is doing the touching?* If (as we may normally say) a padded slipper or another person or your pet cat happened to be touching your knee, would these particular sensations communicate the source? Do these particular sensations provide direct experience about what is doing the touching?

- Do these particular experiences of touch provide direct experience of any separate physical object at all?

- What would be the difference in the direct experience of touch between (a) an object touching your knee and (b) your knee touching an object? As we saw in the section on the "World", the sense of touch by itself is incapable of verifying a physical object. So how is this case any different?

- In steps (1) and (2), is there any direct experience that sensations arise in the absence of witnessing awareness? Is witnessing awareness ever experienced as being absent?

CASE B: One experience, that of toucher and touched, can't be differentiated

This is an interesting scenario. The case of a "hand touching a knee" may just be directly experienced as one undifferentiated case of touching. You may not be able to distinguish a "touching" part from a "being touched" part going by the direct experience of touch alone. In everyday life you don't have to. In everyday life, you may rely on other cues to tell yourself what is happening. You may rely on belief, vision, imagination and cultural teaching to conclude that the hand is touching the knee. But is anything like that *really* happening? Is that kind of independence and duality and separation *really* your experience? That is exactly why we are taking an ultra-close look through direct experience.

If, in your direct experience, there is no distinction between a "touching" part and a "being touched" part, it is perfectly OK. Again, there are no wrong answers in direct experience. If you have already done the experiments for external objects in the "World" section of this book, then you have already understood how there are no separate and independent objects given in direct sensory experience in the first place. So it is not the case that the sense of touch is being inaccurate!

Is the body any different from these other objects, just because it seems ... "closer"? Let's see!

- Going just by this arising sense of touch and not by memory, belief, habit or visualization, is there any evidence of a body being touched? Does the sensation itself communicate information that a body is the object being touched? If it seems like the sensation is communicating this information, just what part of the sensation is saying it?

- In fact, is there any direct evidence that this arising sensation is being caused by any object at all? Keeping just to this sensation, is there any direct experience of anything that it is a sensation "of"? Do you experience the sensation to be referring or pointing to anything apart from itself?

- Is there any direct experience that a body is doing the touching? If it seems to be so, then just what part of the sensation is communicating this information? How can just a sensation (and not a belief or theory or sentence) provide direct experience about something doing the touching?

- In step (2) (where the "hand is taken away from the knee"), is there anything directly experienced by the sense of touch to be missing?

- Is there ever any direct experience of a sensation that is arising in the absence of witnessing awareness?

- Is witnessing awareness ever experienced to be absent?

To Do On Your Own

Perform the touching experiment on different parts of the body: touch your hand, arm, chest, face, back of your head, back of the neck, hips, legs, feet.

Perform these same kinds of experiments with another person touching the same places on your body.

Perform a touching experiment where you sense the body being touched by the chair you are sitting in, or a wall you are leaning against, or the ground you are standing on or walking on.

Is there anything in direct experience that is experienced apart from (or in the absence of) witnessing awareness?

Is witnessing awareness ever directly experienced to be absent from experience?

Is there anything directly experienced to be the body other than awareness?

Hearing, Smelling And Tasting The Body

Hearing, smelling and tasting are not dominant senses (compared to seeing and touching) when it comes to how we think of the body. So we can spend less time in these senses than we did for seeing and touching.

The body arises as sounds, odors and flavors:

- **Sounds:** talking, walking, breathing, coughing, sneezing, swallowing, burping, bones creaking and joints cracking.

- **Odors:** including those associated with sweat, sex, freshly washed hair, nervousness, "morning breath," flatulence, before and after a much-needed shower, illness. The various bodily fluids are often considered parts of the body, and they arise as distinct odors as well.

- **Flavors:** including those associated with the various bodily fluids, as well as those arising as the roof of the mouth, the teeth, lips, skin, etc.

What we will investigate is whether these sounds, odors and flavors are direct evidence of a body that is independently existent and separate from awareness. Are they directly experienced as originating from the body?

Experiment 8 – Hearing, Smelling And Tasting The Body

Purpose – Discovering how the body is experienced to arise in hearing, smell and taste.

Objects needed – A chair.

Setup – Sit quietly in the chair.

The Experiments – Begin with the Heart Opener so that you can establish yourself as the open clear spaciousness of awareness. Close your eyes.

1 **Sounds:** Start with your mouth closed and your teeth together. Gently click your teeth together 3 times. Concentrate on *just the sound*, not the sensation of touch. Pause for 5 seconds. Repeat as necessary. You may also try the sound of clapping your hands, snapping your fingers, sniffing, swallowing, slapping your knee, cracking your joints, emitting a long "OM!" sound, etc.

Concentrate on just the sounds that arise. There may be other sensations that are noticeable, but they have either been examined or will be examined separately. In this experiment, we are investigating just the sounds that we would normally think are caused by the body.

2 Odors: Raise your hand to your nose. Sniff the palm of your hand 3 times. Concentrate on *just the odor*, not the sensations associated with breathing. Pause for several inhalations. Repeat as necessary. You may also try the odor of your breath by cupping your hand over your mouth and nose, and sniffing as you exhale. Or sniffing under your arm, or smelling your hair if it is long enough!

Concentrate on just the odors that arise. There may be other sensations, but investigate just the odors themselves. We will look into whether they are experienced as originating in the body or being caused by the body.

3 Flavors: Place your tongue against the roof of your mouth for 5 seconds. Concentrate on *just the flavor* for 5 seconds. Remove your tongue from the roof of your mouth for 5 seconds. Repeat as necessary. You may also try the flavor of your teeth, the gums under your lip, outside your mouth above your upper lip, your hand or arm, etc.

Concentrate on just the flavors that arise. There may be other sensations, especially since the tongue is thought to be able to perceive tactile sensations as well as gustatory (flavor) sensations. But in this experiment we are concentrating just on the flavors.

Inquiry into sounds, odors and flavors – As in all our explorations of the "body as object," we are treating the body as another supposedly external object like a chair or an orange. So we will inquire into these questions: do the sensations that arise provide direct experience of a body that causes the sensations? Are there even any separate sensations directly experienced at all? Is there anything directly experienced as separate and apart from witnessing awareness?

- **Sounds:** From step (1) above, do the clicking sounds that arise provide direct experience of any object that causes the clicking? Do you experience any sounds apart from hearing? If not, this means that a sound is not there to be heard. If so, then how can it be that you actually "hear a sound"? Wherever there is sound, there is hearing. Do you experience the arising of hearing in the absence of witnessing awareness? Is there anything directly experienced to be present other than witnessing awareness?

- **Odors**: From step (2) above, does the "hand" odor that arises provide direct experience of any object that causes the odor? Is there direct experience of a hand within the odor? Do you experience any odor apart from the sense of smell? If not, this means that an odor is not there to be smelled. If so, then how can it be that you actually "smell an odor"? The same lack of independence applies to the sense of smell. Do you experience the arising of the sense of smell in the absence of witnessing awareness? Is there anything directly experienced to be present other than witnessing awareness?

- **Flavors**: From step (3) above, does the "roof of the mouth" flavor that arises provide direct experience of any object that causes the flavor? Is there direct experience of a mouth within the flavor itself? Do you experience any flavor apart from the sense of taste? If not, this means that any flavor is not there to be tasted. If so, then how can it be that you actually "taste a flavor"? The same lack of independence applies to the sense of taste. Do you experience the arising of the sense of taste in the absence of witnessing awareness? Is there anything directly experienced to be present other than witnessing awareness?

The Body As Object – Conclusion

The experiments we have just done have actually confirmed the insights and realizations gained in Part 1 – The World. That is, there is no direct experience of the body as a physical object among other physical objects in the world. The body, like the world, arises as what seem like sensations apprehended by the various senses. But upon close examination, we see that the sensations themselves are not experienced independently of the various sensory modalities.

If we were ever able to experience anything existing objec͏ti͏͏͏
would experience it existing apart from witnessin͏͏
we would be able to verify that witnessing awar͏
it. But our experience is never like this. Witnessi͏
already the nature of our experience. We never get
ence anything existing in the absence of witnessi͏
because awareness is always the nature of experien͏

If this is fully understood, the insight cuts through the very basis for a supposedly external physical world and perishable physical body. That is, we never experience the objectivity of the world or the body, because we never experience the objectivity of sensations. We think we "see the world" or "touch the body," but visual colors and tactile textures are never experienced as independent of vision and touch, respectively. This means that we never see a color that is present and waiting to be seen. We never touch a texture that is there to be touched.

The arising of color and texture are never experienced as the coming and going of pre-existing things. They are not experienced as happening *through* sensing. Sensing is not a neutral or independent medium which first exists and then transmits color, texture and other sensations. Once we consider our experience directly, we come to understand that sensing is the word we give to the arising of these sensations. For example, arising of color isn't something that happens through vision. In direct experience, we don't find a pre-existing vision which serves as a receiver for colors that arise. It's sort of the other way around. Colors arise, and they seem very different from textures and sounds. So we think of the arising of color as a process and we call it "vision." And this is the same whether it is the world or the body that we normally think is "seen." There is no independence or separate existence in sensation. Sensory objects are not "out there" waiting to be sensed. They are also not "in here" as sensed or perceived objects.

The sensory modalities themselves are not independent either. Seeing, touching and hearing are not objects that are experienced as pre-existing, which then happen to be apprehended by witnessing awareness. There is never any experiential access to the faculty of seeing other than through witnessing awareness, so there is no way to verify the independent existence of seeing. We may think we witness seeing as an activity or ability that's already taking place. But we never experience it this way. In witnessing awareness, sometimes seeing seems to arise. But seeing is never experienced apart from witnessing awareness. So we never "catch seeing in the act" of being found out by witnessing awareness.

This is why it is often said that awareness is closer than the palm of hand. It is the very nature of us.

The Body As Feeler

> *My body is unique. It's the only object in the universe*
> *where I **feel** it if it is touched. When my body is touched*
> *in a certain way, I feel pain. **What could be more real***
> ***than this?** When a car or a table is touched, I don't feel*
> *it. Even when another person is touched, I don't feel it.*
> *I feel it, when my body is touched, and when my body is*
> *touched, I feel it. This is what makes me feel that I am*
> *the body.*

Seeker's comment

Am I a body that feels things? This sense of a unique connection with the body is something that most seekers will encounter sooner or later. We normally look at it like this: we don't know exactly how *other* people feel when *their* body is touched. We know *exactly* how it feels when *we* are touched. And as for non-sentient objects like rivers and rocks, we doubt if they feel anything at all. No wonder we feel like we are the body, or at least intimately connected with the body!

Let us now look at the body as if from the inside. Direct experience will show us that the body, just like the rest of the world, is not even an object, but rather nothing other than awareness, the body of light, which is the truth of the self and the world, of existence itself. The body is never verified as a separate apparatus with the unique and vulnerable ability to feel things.

In The Everyday Sense

And even before we delve into what is verified in direct experience, we can see that there are some problems with our seeker's comment.

One problem is very telling. Notice the connection the speaker makes between pain and reality. "...I feel pain. What could be more real than this?" This is quite common. We say, "Get real!" when we are trying to get someone to accept something painful or unpleasant. We don't say it to someone who can't believe they won the lottery. This tells us something about the goals that we may bring with us into our self-inquiry.

One friend of mine defined enlightenment as the ability to withstand torture without feeling any pain. His goal was to keep the separate self in the picture, but allow it to feel only pleasant things.

But nondual inquiry is much more radical than this, and my friend realized it as he continued. It is not a matter of keeping what you want and losing what you don't want. Rather, nondual inquiry leads to the global and joyful discovery that there is no separate body, no pain in the first place, and that the reality of our experience is always and already the beauty and sweetness of awareness.

The speaker assumes a correlation between their own body being touched as a physical object and the arising of a feeling or sensation. But this correlation is only assumed, and it breaks down in practice:

- **"When another person is touched, I don't feel it."** Not always true. In some cases, very sympathetic people do feel it when they see or intuit another person being touched who is close to their heart.

- **"When my body is touched, I feel it."** Not always true. There are cases of numbness, inattention, sleep, trance confusion or neurological disorders when you can be touched without feeling it.

There are also cases where you can "feel it" even if your body is not touched. This includes cases of dreams, memories, vivid imagination and phantom limb pain.

These exceptions to the assumed correlation between touching and feeling offer an opportunity. It is the possibility of something much more vast and global than a separate physical body.

And In Direct Experience

If you have been following the course of this book, then by this point you have discovered that the body isn't an object in the first place. Just like other objects in "the world," it is not physical and does not take up space. We have looked very closely and have found no causal interactions between the body and other objects. We haven't even found any objects. No matter how closely we looked, we haven't been able to find anything like "a person tapping my shoulder."

The body is thought to be able to feel lots of different kinds of sensations and objects. In this section we will investigate to see if this is actually our direct experience. We will look deeply at whether it is truly our experience to be an object that has various kinds of sensations.

What Does The Body Feel?

The body is usually thought to be able to feel many kinds of things: sensations, pains and pleasure, placement and position, itches, tickles, twitches and contractions, hunger, thirst, satiation, fullness, movement, stiffness, suppleness, balance and imbalance, tiredness and excitement.

This list could go on and on. We doubt whether chairs and tables have these feelings, but we're sure that **we** do! This certainly is part of what makes us feel unique.

But is it really our experience to be a feeler? Let's take a close look!

First of all, we've already realized that we never experience any object as a *felt* thing. We discovered that the body is not a separate, experienced *object*. We are here inquiring whether we experience the body as a feeler, a unique *subject*. We'll start with sensing.

Sensing

A biologist may say that sensing depends on the biological apparatus. We all know how this theory goes. We are not offering a competing theory. What we are doing is this – without trying to invalidate the contributions of biological science, we are merely investigating what we directly experience ourselves to be.

What happens if we don't find that direct experience agrees with biology? Are we wrong? Is biology wrong? Not at all! Biology is a certain "song" with a particular melody and purpose. Our self-inquiry is another song with a different melody. Its purpose is to free us from suffering by helping us discover who we truly are.

Experiment 9 – Is The Body An Object That Senses?

Purpose – Discovering whether we directly experience the body to perform sensing.

Objects needed – A chair, table, sliced orange or apple.

Setup – Sit quietly in the chair.

The Experiment – Close your eyes. Begin with the Heart Opener so that you can establish yourself as the open clear spaciousness of awareness.

1 Do you really see? Allow yourself to "see" the table. In the direct experience of color arising, do you catch your body in the act as something that performs the seeing? Sticking with seeing alone, do you see a pair of eyes seeing color? In direct experience, do you see, hear, feel, smell or taste the seeing? Do you see a body part that is directly experienced as a seeing thing? Do you see a seer?

2 Do you really hear? Close your eyes. Allow yourself to "hear" the ambient noises inside or outside the room. It could be traffic sounds from outside, or a refrigerator, TV, air conditioner or heater, etc. Sticking with hearing alone, do you hear a set of ears? Do you hear anything performing the activity of hearing? Does a hearer arise in direct experience?

3 Do you really touch? Close your eyes. Very slowly, lower your hand to the tabletop until it "makes contact." Somewhere in the direct experience of touch (which can include texture, hardness, warmth/coolness, dryness/moistness, etc.), is there direct evidence that a hand is doing the touching? Is an object such as a "toucher" arising in direct experience as that which is doing the touching? Is a function of touching being touched?

4 Are you really able to smell? With a fork, lift the sliced orange or apple to your nose. Take a whiff. In the fragrance that arises, is there any direct evidence that a nose is doing the smelling? Is there any fragrance of "smelling" as a function that arises in direct experience?

5 Are you really able to taste? Now take a bite of the orange or apple. In the various sensations that arise – flavor, moistness, hardness/softness, movement – do you taste a taster? Does the tongue catch the tongue in the act of tasting? Is there something evident that is the direct experience of a taster?

Pain

At home at night in the dark, I'm walking to the kitchen. All of a sudden – BOOM! I see stars, I feel the acute onset of the most unpleasant gnawing, pulsating pain. I hobble over to the light switch and find that I have hit my shin on the coffee table that someone moved earlier in the evening. What could be more real than this?

Pain is the show-stopper for many people. Pain is real, they say. It hurts. When it's intense, it hurts more. People have told me that for nonduality to be as real as their experience of pain, nonduality would have to remove their pain. Otherwise, what good is it?

That's the bad rap that "reality" gets. The unpleasant is the real. The pleasant is called "dreaming." No wonder pain is so often supplied as the most "real" kind of experience! There are many different forms of feeling that are called "pain." The feeling can be of many different types:

- an ache such as a headache, stomach ache, toothache, muscle or bone ache

- a bruising feeling (the coffee table)

- a burning feeling

- a scraping, rasping feeling

- a stinging feeling

And the pain seems much worse (and much more real) if it is both intense and unexpected. It can be followed by a feeling of indignation, such as "How dare the coffee table do that to me (without telling me)! We can even blame the coffee table, holding it causally and morally responsible for our situation, as though the coffee table had plotted against us. All of this adds to the overall feeling of discomfort.

However, notice this. These elements are not the direct experience *of* the pain, but various thoughts and feelings *about* the pain. They are intimately connected with the quality of our experience surrounding this painful episode, but they are not the direct experience of pain itself. For example, indignation and feelings of blame are mental assertions and emotional attitudes. The intensity is like a measured comparative aspect to the pain, analogous to the saturation or intensity of a color. The unexpectedness of the pain is a mental conclusion based on the fact that there was not a thought about pain immediately previously to the onset of the pain.

Of course, all these elements add to the general feeling of discomfort, and they are all based on thoughts and feelings about pain. We will examine these aspects in Part 3 of this book, where we examine the mind. In this section we will examine the direct experience of the pain itself. What we are searching for in this investigation is direct experience bearing on this:

Q: In the direct experience of pain, do we experience a body feeling pain?

We might say,

A: Of course, I have direct experience of the body feeling the pain! I feel my sore shin, and I see that it has a red bump that is turning blue minute by minute! I am directly observing the body feeling pain!

But let's take a closer look.

Experiment 10 – Pain

Purpose – Discovering whether pain establishes that the body is objectively feeling something.

Let's do a thought-experiment about pain. Have you ever barked your shin on a table, stubbed your toe or bashed your knee into the computer under your desk? Most people have. So think back on one of those times....

Cautionary note: If you suspect that you may have any medical or psychological issues involving pain, then consult your physician or therapist before conducting the following exercise.

---

1 Remember the direct experience of the pain: Close your eyes and attend to the (remembered) direct experience of the pain itself. You may have experienced a flare of gnawing, aching discomfort. It may have come and gone in waves. Even when that discomfort was at its highest, did the feeling come pre-packaged with a label saying that the pain was happening in the shin, the toe or in the body? Is there any body attached to the pain? Actually, many people have the experience that in very deep pain there seems to be nothing arising other than the pain itself.

2 The thought about the pain is not the pain: There might have been a thought that said, "I couldn't possibly be feeling this unless it were happening to my body," but notice that this was a thought *about* the pain and not the pain itself. A thought about pain is not the direct experience of pain – it is more like the direct experience of a thought. Similarly, if the pain seems intense, surprising, worse than 90% of the other pains you have experienced, etc., notice that these are also thoughts not included in the pain itself.

3 Can you really *see the pain*? So now (in memory), look at the area on the body that seems affected by the pain. In memory, let's say that a red or blue color arises in/as the seeing. In the direct experience of vision, what makes this particular color equal to pain? What color IS pain? Poetically it is depicted with red to symbolize blood or green to symbolize envy or other emotional distress. But in the direct experience of the color itself, what is your direct visual experience that amounts to pain? Does the color carry a label that says "pain"? Do you see the color feeling pain? There may be thoughts arising that say, "This redness is the same thing as the unpleasant feeling.

That is how I am seeing the pain." But notice that this is a series of thoughts about the pain, and not included in the pain itself. If the direct experience of pain does not include the experience of a body feeling the pain, vision does not include it, and a thought does not include the experience either, then when you combine all three modes of experience together, you still get no direct experience of a body as a feeler. Zero + zero + zero = zero.

4 After all, what makes it "pain" in the first place? Even the pain doesn't come self-identified. It doesn't announce itself as "pain." The label comes from a thought, which, again, is not direct experience of the pain. So even the "pain" is not "pain" in direct experience. It surely seems like something, but any particular thing always depends on an attribution by thought.

5 Is the pain separate from witnessing awareness? This is more subtle. Is the pain something you experience as apart from awareness? Is it something pre-existing that awareness just happens to discover? Do you have some way of experiencing the pain that does not involve witnessing awareness at all? That is how you would be able to apprehend the pain-in-itself to prove that witnessing awareness grasps it.

Another way to think about this is by analogy. You know how we normally think about physical objects. Before we began our inquiry, we probably thought that physical objects are completely independent of perception and awareness. They seem not to need our perception in order to exist. So is the pain like this? For example, let's consider a house cat that you see in one room and then another. The cat (we usually think) can be present sometimes and absent sometimes (because it is present somewhere else). We normally think the cat exists even if it is not presently experienced.

But is the pain like this? Is the pain ever experienced as existing outside of awareness? In other words, is the pain ever experienced as a separate, independent thing that experience discovers? In other words, do you ever have direct experience of pain when witnessing awareness is absent?

6 Is it really true that pain should not occur? The subjunctive form "should" is used in evaluations and normative statements. "You should call your mother," or "I should have a better life." But other than an evaluative claim and its attendant concepts and standards, where does this "should" come from? Is there anything in the pain itself that communicates an evaluation? Even though we may prefer to have our dentistry with anesthesia rather than without, and believe a painless procedure is better than a painful one, is it the pain itself that communicates this preferentiality? Or is the preferentiality a belief?

Another way to look at it is this – it's not always the case that we want to be pain-free. Consider being a cyclist practicing to climb hills faster. The muscles and lungs seem to burn! Athletes use the information from this pain as an indication that more training is needed. Pain can be a valuable signal, and not everyone wants to wish it out of existence. So is there anything in the direct experience of this burning sensation that establishes that right here, right now, it should not occur?

7 Is the pain anything other than awareness? This is a continuation of (5). Try as much as you can – can you come up with any experience in which pain is present, but witnessing awareness is not present for the pain to appear to? Whenever pain is, awareness is there. Whenever pain is not, awareness is still there. Awareness is the only experienced common factor, whether the pain is arising or not. This means that there is nothing in the direct experience of pain other than awareness.

Conclusion To Sensing And Pain – And Pleasure

The senses of vision, touch, hearing and the experience of pain are often thought to be the most definitive features that prove reality. They have the greatest "reality effect" (see Part 1 – The World). But we have just discovered that even with these kinds of show-stopper experiences, there is simply no direct evidence of a body existing as a feeler. Direct experience never includes "the body as a feeler of direct experience."

Under "pain" we can include all sorts of discomfort that we usually say involves the body: feeling very hungry, feeling too full, feeling stiff in the joints or muscles, having the "must go to the bathroom" feeling, feeling exhausted. You can try these same inquiries into your direct experience when any of these experiences arise. Do they carry with them direct evidence that a body is doing the feeling?

We did not examine pleasure in the same way, because pleasure is not too much of an issue — so often it has a much smaller reality effect. But you are free to investigate on your own. There are many available pleasures: the first few sips of cool water when you are thirsty. A bite of your favorite dessert. An orgasm. A great backrub. My mother used to rub my forehead to help me go to sleep — it felt fantastic. The touch of fine velvet. Pulling on a pair of comfortable old jeans or sneakers. You can do the very same kind of inquiry. And you will make the same kind of discovery. Nothing in the direct experience of pleasure brings with it the direct experience that a body is feeling pleasure.

And, of course, by this point in the book, if you have come all the way with me so far, we have already discovered that the body is not an object in the first place. So it is incapable of conveying experience. But it is helpful to examine the sense of the body's reality from this different angle, to see whether we have direct experience of the body as a feeling object. In either case, the more deeply we look, the more we discover only awareness!

But what about some other kinds of experience? Let's examine something a bit different — the senses of positionality and movement.

Positionality

Do we experience the body as something occupying a certain position or posture? Does the seeming existence of movement prove that we are (in) a body that moves and changes position? This is called "proprioception" in neuroscience and cognitive psychology. Let's take a look.

Cautionary note: If you suspect that you may have any medical or psychological issues involving pain, then consult your physician or therapist before conducting the following exercise.

Experiment 11 – Is Your Arm In A Certain Position?

Let's try an exercise to see whether the position of the body provides direct experience of the presence of a body as a feeler.

Purpose – Discovering whether the body's position proves that the body is really a feeler.

Objects needed – A chair and table.

Setup – Sit quietly in the chair with your hands resting easily in your lap.

The Experiment – Notice that it calls for your eyes to be closed. Since the steps can't be read while your eyes are closed, read through the steps first to get a feel for the sequence. Then try the steps that call for your eyes to be closed. Of course, you can open your eyes at any time if you wish, and especially if you need to take another look at the steps! Begin with the Heart Opener so that you can establish yourself as the open clear spaciousness of awareness.

1 Do you experience your arm being out in front? Close your eyes. Rest your dominant arm comfortably on the table, pointed straight out in front of you. Don't go by the sense of touch (i.e., from the "arm touching the table"), as we've done that already. Don't go by a visual image of an arm pointing out to the front; we've done that too. Rather, try to go just by the positional feeling, the sense that your arm is in a certain position. Does this positional experience carry with it the direct experience that the feeling is coming from your arm?

2 Do you experience your arm to be bent? Still with your eyes closed, bend your arm into a comfortable angle. You are trying to focus directly on the sense of position, and not on the sense of touch or vision. In this way, going by the sense of position alone, do you have direct evidence that it is (what you would normally consider to be) your arm that is in a position, or that your **arm** is generating or communicating the feeling? Is this feeling labeled with the concepts "arm" or "angle"? In other words, does the sense of position by itself give you direct experience which supports your usual belief that you actually have a part of the body called an arm?

3 Add a sense of effort. With your eyes still closed, raise your arm to the side until it is angled between 45° and 90° out from your trunk. Let it remain there while you ask the following questions. If you need a bit of rest, then return your hand to your lap and try again a moment later. In addition to the sense of positionality that we explored in steps (1) and (2), there is probably another sort of experience that is very evident. That is the sense of tiredness, effort, or even a burning sensation.

We would normally say that this sense is "in the shoulder," but we have already discovered that there is **no shoulder for the sensation to be in.** Rather, it is a sense that is associated by thought with another sense (thought?) that gets labeled "shoulder." The outcome will be another thought, "This is beginning to hurt my shoulder." But all these thoughts are not direct positional experience. They are thoughts purporting to be *about* the positional experience. We will cover thoughts in Part 3 - The Mind. But for now, let us stick just to the senses of positionality and effort. Going by these senses, is there any direct evidence that it is the *arm* that is feeling these things?

4 Return to the initial position. With your eyes still closed, return your arm to your side so that your hand is resting comfortably in your lap. Continuing to go just by the sense of positionality (and the sense of the lack of effort!), look for any direct experience that it is your *arm* that is feeling the experience. Do any of these experiences prove an arm?

To Do On Your Own

There is abundant opportunity to inquire into positionality, because your body always seems to be in one position or another. You can inquire while sitting, standing or lying down. You can do mini-exercises like the following:

- **Sitting in a chair** – Sit in a chair looking straight forward. Position your head so that you are looking parallel to the floor or ground, and shut your eyes. Do you have direct positional evidence that it is your head that is positioned just so? Now turn your head slightly to the right. Do you have direct experience that it is your head that is in this position?

- **Lying in bed** – Lie on your back with your legs straight out, feet together. Do you feel the experience of the position of your legs and feet? Now spread your feet apart, keeping your legs straight. Do you feel the direct experience of this position? Now bend your knees by bringing your feet in closer to your hips. Do you directly feel this position? In these different positions, do you have direct experience that it is your feet and legs that are positioned just so?

- **Standing in line** – The next time you are caught in a line at the bank or grocery store, investigate whether the sense of standing, of being upright, includes the direct experience that it is the body that's doing the standing.

You experience the positional sense as an arising in awareness; the question to investigate is whether the positional sense proves the presence of a body that feels these things. If the positional sense does not prove the body in this way, then this can open you up to the possibility that the only direct experience is awareness itself.…

Movement

> Sometimes I wonder, "Why is that Frisbee getting
> bigger?"
> … and then it hits me.

Let's add the sense of movement to the sense of positionality.

Experiment 12a – Is Your Body Moving With The Chair?

Purpose – Discovering whether the sense of movement establishes that the body is truly feeling or perceiving anything objective.

Objects needed – A chair that can roll smoothly. A smooth floor in a room. A friend or associate.

Setup – Find a room that has a smooth floor with enough free space so that the chair can roll side to side. Ideally the chair can be positioned to roll side to side in front of a wall. If the room allows it, position the chair so that it is facing the wall. Sit quietly in the chair. Have another person ready to push the chair from side to side along the wall.

The Experiment – Sit comfortably in the chair facing the wall. Begin with the Heart Opener.

1 With a soft focus, look at the wall. Have your associate slowly and steadily move the chair (with you in it) to your left or right, a few feet or more. Then have your associate move the chair back in the other direction. Keep your head facing forward. Try not to move your neck. Try not to move your eyes either, as you would if you were tracking a particular spot on the wall. Instead, keep your focus soft and open as the chair is pushed left and right.

2 What is your direct visual experience? There are a lot of sensations that arise in this situation. In this step, attend only to the visual sensations. Based on visual evidence alone, is there any evidence that you are moving? Is there any visual evidence that you have a body that is moving through space? There is a sense of colors moving right or left, but is there any direct experience that you have a body, that you are a body, or that you are moving?

3 Attend to the other sensations as well. While this chair is moving side to side, there will be sounds arising, as well as sensations of touch and kinesthetic and proprioceptive sensations from what we would normally call "vibrations," as well as inertia, stillness and the absence of sensation. Allow these sensations to be attended to in addition to visual experience. Is there now any direct evidence that you are a body or that you are moving? Of course, there might be a thought that says, "My body is moving towards the right." But is that the direct experience from touch or kinesthesia or proprioception? Is it possible that the body-notion is not given in direct experience, but is merely a thought?

Experiment 12b – Is Your Body Moving With The Car?

Objects needed – A car. A friend or associate with a driver's license.

Setup – The setup is similar to some of the experiments from Douglas Harding (author of On Having No Head, see: www.headless.org/experiments.htm for more information). But in our case, the inquiry is different. Have a friend drive you around town while you sit in the passenger's seat (with the door locked for safety) and look out the window.

The Experiment – Sit comfortably in the seat. Begin with the Heart Opener.

1 With a soft focus, look out the passenger-side window. Keep your head and eyes still and your vision softly focused. Don't try to track an "object as it goes by."

2 What is your direct visual experience? First, attend only to the visual sensations. Keeping to the visual only, is there any evidence that you are moving? Is there any visual evidence that you have a body that is moving through space? There is a sense of colors moving right or left, but is there any direct experience that you have a body, that you are a body, or that you are moving?

3 Attend to the other sensations as well. While "in this car moving down the street," you may experience sounds, bumps, jolts, vibrations, turns, starts and stops, in addition to the colors. Not going by thought, memory or imagination but by direct experience only, is there now any direct evidence that you are a body that is moving?

Conclusion To The Body As Feeler

We have looked at the body as if from the outside and found it to arise as visual, tactile and other sensations. In this way, the body is no different from a table or chair. It arises as sensations, which are never separate from sensing. Sensing is never separate from witnessing awareness. Witnessing awareness is always present, never absent. It's the only factor that is common to situations in which there **aren't** sensations as well as situations in which there **are** arisings (sensations?). Awareness is always and already your common experience.

We have also looked at the body as if from the inside, as something that supposedly feels. And we have found that there is no direct evidence that the body stands apart among objects as a special object that is able to sense and perceive and feel. All of our direct sensory and perceptual experience is "of" sensations coming and going in witnessing awareness. At no time does direct experience establish a body that conveys direct experience. The body as a separate vehicle of sensation has been surprisingly absent during our experiments into direct experience. We saw how direct experience always takes place in perfect, free openness. Experience is like that. Awareness is like that. Indeed, they are the same thing!

The Body As Container

Does the body contain awareness? Is awareness *in* the body?

- *I know that I am awareness and everything is awareness, but why can't I see your thoughts?*

- *Yes, there is nothing outside of awareness, but then why can't I see the Great Wall of China?*

- *You and I are looking at a tree. Are we seeing the same tree (thing?)?*

- *You and I are looking at each other. Who is appearing to whom?*

This is one of the stickiest issues confronted sooner or later by people doing direct inquiry. It's the sense that awareness is somehow limited to what (we normally say) can be perceived by this particular body. We feel as though awareness has contents inside it, and that awareness is somehow inside the body. Or at least closely **related to** the body. It may be felt that awareness is **in** the body, or something that **animates** or **takes the shape of** the body. Awareness may even be felt to extend beyond the body – it can seem to constitute the sensory field and extend as far as you can see or hear. But even so, most inquirers have the distinct feeling that awareness has a home base in or around the body, and that there are distant areas, that, at least for the moment, lie beyond awareness.

Thinking of awareness in this way gives rise to questions like the ones above.

These questions depend on a set of related assumptions.

- Awareness is closely linked to this body, probably inside it.

- Awareness is personal, one per person.

- It seems that the world is like a "fall" from awareness.

- Something can be in awareness or out of it.

- It seems that most of the world resides outside the container of awareness.

- Something can be outside the container of **my** awareness but within the container of **your** awareness.

The container metaphor conditions a great deal about how we think of ourselves and our experience. We feel containment in at least two ways:

1 The body or mind contains awareness.

2 Awareness contains objects of perception and cognition.

If we operate according to these assumptions, it can seem that we are caught in a limited bubble of awareness that needs to somehow burst in order for us to reach global awareness. And as long as we see awareness in terms of containers, we will tend to think of even global awareness as a container. A huge, universal container perhaps, but a container nevertheless. This makes it very natural to suspect that just maybe there can be things happening outside this universal container. And this leaves open the anxiety-provoking possibility that separation is part of the reality of things.

But we will discover how containment and separation are *never* our experience.

But before we do, let's spend a little time reflecting on why the container metaphor is so powerful and prevalent. It has been part of the dualistic notion of the person in Western culture for thousands of years.

The Container Metaphor In Western Culture

The soul is a helpless prisoner chained hand and foot in the body.

Phaedo by Plato (427-347 BCE)

The body is the tomb of the soul.

Cratylus by Plato

Thou hast clothed me in skin and flesh, and hast fenced me with bones and sinew.

Book of Job

You must know that your body is a temple of the Holy Spirit, who is within....

1 Corinthians 6:19

In the 17th century, the container metaphor gained scientific and philosophical dominance. Science, mechanics and optics had given rise to a geometrical, mechanistic model of the universe. René Descartes (1596-1650) added a sharply defined mind-body dualism to this worldview. Descartes has been called the father of modern philosophy, and his influence on the Western model of the mind is stronger than Freud's.

A Ghost In A Machine

Descartes desired to have a rock-solid foundation upon which our knowledge of the world could be based. What could we know even if everything was in doubt? Descartes theorized that we could know that we are a thinking thing, and that this is one thing that cannot be doubted. If we have a physical body, it would contain this non-physical substance. He visualized the soul or the self as an unextended and unmoving non-physical substance inside a machine-like container.

Descartes described the self as a thinking thing with an inside and an outside:

> *I think therefore I am.*

Discourse on Method (1637)

> *Strictly speaking, then, I am simply a thing that thinks*
> *— a mind, or soul, or intellect, or reason, these being*
> *words whose meaning I have only just come to know.*
> *Still, I am a real, existing thing.*

Meditations on First Philosophy (1641)

> *... even if the objects of my sensory experience and*
> *imagination don't exist outside me, still sensory*
> *perception and imagination themselves, considered*
> *simply as mental events, certainly do occur in me.*

Meditations on First Philosophy (1641)

Cartesian Anxiety

Descartes' model of the mind became prominent. Separation through containment worked its way into how the West regarded the mind, thinking and awareness. Because of the absolute difference between the non-material thinking substance and its material container, a deep metaphysical anxiety was created: how could the mind ever be sure of what was outside the mind?

Descartes theorized that we could not be sure. Because all we could be sure of was that we think, and therefore exist, we could never be sure about anything external to the mind. In his **Meditations on First Philosophy**, Descartes realized that with this bifurcation between an inside and an outside, the inside could never perceive the outside clearly or with certainty:

> But I used also to believe that my ideas came from
> things outside that resembled them in all respects.
> Indeed, I believed this for so long that I wrongly came
> to think that I perceived it clearly. In fact, it was false;
> or anyway, if it was true, it was not thanks to the
> strength of my perceptions.

This metaphysical anxiety was dramatized with the notion of a malicious demon. Descartes wrote that for all we know, a demon is systematically deceiving us into thinking that a world exists when we can never know for sure:

> So I shall suppose that some malicious, powerful,
> cunning demon has done all he can to deceive me ...
> I shall think that the sky, the air, the earth, colors,
> shapes, sounds and all external things are merely
> dreams that the demon has contrived as traps for my
> judgment.

We think our ideas about external things come from those things themselves, but how do we know? Descartes' own solution to this problem would not work for most people today. The answer is found through faith in God. God would never deceive us or let a cunning demon deceive us. Therefore we can rest assured that when we think our ideas come from things themselves God ensures that this is really true.

Anxiety And Nonduality

These days the inquirer into nonduality is in an ironic position. The dualistic container metaphor is still very much with us. We've inherited the alienation and anxiety of the metaphor, but we usually don't accept the religious solution that comforted Descartes. So what's the nondual inquirer to do? This is one of the most challenging roadblocks to realization.

This sort of metaphysically-defined anxiety has more down-to-earth effects as well. It is not uncommon to feel trapped inside one's head or body. It is not uncommon to feel cut off and separated from the world in general or from other people. It can feel as though the world is an alien place, or that we are trapped behind a screen, or within some kind of container.

Seeing Through The Metaphor

Why call the container notion a "metaphor"? A metaphor is a description of one thing in terms appropriate to another. With the container metaphor, we think of awareness and experience in terms appropriate to physical objects such as bowls, barrels and buckets. These physical containers have insides and outsides. There is also structure: between the insides and outsides are surfaces that separate them. The surfaces also give shape to the containers and allow us to distinguish one container from another.

When this is applied to experience, the problem is almost inevitable. We have taken the container metaphor as a literal description of our experience. We come to really believe that our experience has an inside and an outside. We think that there are surfaces or walls between one experiencer and another. We regard this as how things really are. We really believe it. The sense of separation ensues, resulting in suffering.

But when looked at directly, experience simply does not have any of these physicalistic or containing elements. There is simply no literal truth in the containment of awareness.

One way we can get a handle on this is to realize that the body is not a physical object to begin with. Sure, there are thoughts that say the body is a physical object. But we have already seen that in direct experience there is nothing physical to the body whatsoever. This includes the head, the skull and the brain. They are arisings in awareness. Arisings aren't physical. *If the body is not physical, how can it contain anything?*

Looking For Containment

We will investigate the nature of our experience to try to verify whether containment is the truth. In direct experience, is there containment? We will discover that direct experience is totally free of containment. Thus, we see through the metaphor and are freed from its grip.

Let's review some of the consequences of containment, so we'll know what to look for. When we think of cups, bottles, tanks and other containers, what features do they have?

- **Inside vs. outside:** If I am the container, then, of course, there must be an inside to my awareness vs. outside to my awareness.

- **My container vs. your container:** If I am one container, then you are another one. Each of us would have a separate awareness inside.

- **Containers within containers:** Like Russian babushka dolls, larger containers can contain smaller containers. If I am the container, then these seem like real possibilities: conscious vs. sub-conscious, heart vs. mind, the remembered vs. the forgotten, the desired vs. the feared, etc.

No wonder this gestalt can lead to feelings of separation! Let's look very closely to see whether containment is actually our direct experience.

Experiment 13 – The Tent

Purpose – Discovering whether we directly experience being contained.

Objects needed – Someplace to sit.

The Experiment – Sit comfortably in a chair or on a couch or in a field. Begin with the Heart Opener. Then visualize the following as vividly as you can, in a simple everyday sense. Don't try to be "nondual," but rather visualize as you normally would:

1 Imagine you are on a camping trip with friends. You're inside your tent. You wake up after a nap and look at the inside wall of your tent. You see a vague lighted area around ground level. You smell a very faint hickory-smoke fragrance. You hear muffled voices. And you see indentations moving back and forth on the canvas, as though someone is moving their finger back and forth.

You stick your head out the tent door. Aha! Now you can see the camp fire. You can smell the hickory smoke more vividly. You hear your friends' voices clearly. And you see that a tree branch is scraping the outside wall of the tent. You can check all these impressions by poking your head back in the tent. Yes! You can see the effects on the inside of the tent made by the various activities taking place on the outside of the tent.

2 Look back towards the tent. Look inwards at the door. Notice that you can see the inside of the tent, the outside of the tent and even a canvas border in between. You are looking at a container. You can see inside the container, outside the container and the wall that separates them. Try to visualize this as vividly as you can.

The tent is a very good example of a literal container in the everyday sense. The tent has all the parts needed to contain things. In this case, the tent contains your backpack, your sleeping bag and even your body. You can verify the containment by being inside or outside or standing in the doorway. But does the notion of containment apply to awareness itself?

Experiment 14 – Are You A Tent?

Purpose – Discovering whether we directly experience being a container.

The Experiment – This is a continuation of Experiment 13. This time, examine your experience directly. Try to replicate what you were able to experience with the tent. Does that way of thinking apply to your experience? To awareness?

1 Wherever you are sitting, allow yourself to be open and look around. Allow the sensations of hearing, smelling and touch to arise.

2 Examine your experience for borders. With the help of vision, hearing, smelling and touch, try to verify whether awareness is contained. If awareness is contained, then you should be able to verify the walls of the container. In any way, do you perceive a wall or borders of a container of experience? Do you experience visual sensations to end at a wall or edge? How about auditory, olfactory or tactile sensations? Do you experience them to be bordered by anything that somehow stands in the way? Is your experience structured so that it has a border with other objects beyond the border?

3 Do you perceive or experience an "inside"? Is awareness experienced as being inside anything? Do you see or hear or smell or feel an inside to a container? Do you directly experience that you are inside something? Do you experience that awareness is inside something?

4 Do you perceive an "outside"? Do you experience in any way a container that you could possibly be outside of? (Think of the tent, where you could choose to go inside or outside.) Do you experience the walls from the outside?

5 Do you perceive *any* containers that contain awareness? Let's say that a visual image arises of a person. According to the Cartesian container metaphor, we usually think a person contains an awareness within. But in your own investigation earlier in this book, you were able to discover that a "body" is nothing more than sensations: colors, sounds, textures, etc. So then – do you experience a **color** containing awareness? Do you experience a separate awareness that is somehow being contained by a color or sound or texture? How could that happen? How could it even make sense?

Conclusion To The Container Experiments

You have discovered that containment is not your direct experience. This frees you from taking the terms of the container metaphor as true and accurate pointers to the truth of experience. This is a great opening and great expansion of heart!

Does Awareness Arise From The Brain?

...the pinkish gray meat between our ears produces the richness of experiential awareness.

Stuart Hameroff, from the **Science and Nonduality Conference** website

In college I dissected brains. As an undergrad student, I was even a physiological psychology major. Many people, even those attracted to nondualism, think that the brain is what gives rise to awareness. But is that our direct experience?

Greg

The Brain

Is the brain essential for awareness to exist? Does awareness actually come from brain activity?

The brain is normally thought of as a mass of a certain kind of biological tissue. That is, it is normally thought of as a physical object. As a physical object, it is normally considered as part of the body, which is part of the world.

But when we do inquiry into our own experience, we investigate: How is the brain experienced? How does it arise?

No one sees their own brain doing the seeing. We may "see" and "feel" the brains of other organisms, the way I did in physiological psychology classes in school. We see many images of brains in anatomy classes, images from CAT-scans and X-rays, in textbooks, on computer screens, represented by scopes and meters of different kinds, and on TV shows about doctors and cops.

What arises in all cases is a visual or tactile image. But biologists and physiologists say that the brain is an essential component for sentience. Even many people attracted to nondual teachings agree (see the first quote above).

When scientists are observing "awareness," they look for measurable, quantifiable phenomena, including:

- certain kinds of reactivity to stimuli

- the ability to see, hear, smell, move, etc.

- the ability to speak or give verbal reports

- the ability to recall objects and actions

- the ability to report one's name or location

- the measurements of chemicals in the brain

- the activity of and within neurons, as measured and depicted by various kinds of scientific apparatus

Notice that even though something non-physical like an "ability" is said to be measured, in all these cases, where awareness is categorized, measured and described, the observations and measurements involve physical objects and events. The essential elements are of the same nature as a table and chair, which we have seen are nothing other than awareness.

It is ironic that brain science is so insistent upon its belief that awareness arises from the brain, because the one great (scientifically) unsolved problem for brain science is *how it happens*. Just how does brain chemistry produce awareness? Scientists have not answered this question.

These conceptualizations and measurements mentioned in the list above do not establish that the awareness spoken of by nonduality is a product of the "pinkish gray meat between our ears." In fact, as we will see in Part 3, the very claim that awareness is produced by chemistry is itself a thought, and thoughts are directly experienced as nothing other than awareness.

Awareness Vs. Sentience

Another way to look at the scientist's approach is this. What exactly is measured by the scientists' activities? Is the "awareness" measured by the scientist the very same global, impersonal, non-phenomenal witnessing Awareness that the nondualist talks about? Are the scientists and the nondualists talking about the same thing? What the scientist is measuring in these ways is something infinitely less subtle: it is sentience, the waking state, which in Advaita-Vedanta is called *jagrat avastha*. This waking state is a subtle object associated with an individual person. It comes and goes, alternating with the dream state (*sushupti avastha*) and deep sleep.

As an object, sentience appears to the very same witnessing awareness that is our true nature. The insight that we are "aware" of our waking state or our sentience is a major realization. It establishes that there is something "larger" and more subtle already in place that sentience appears to. But if you stop to consider for a moment, it is totally obvious (most of the time I hope) that you are awake and not in deep sleep.

If you were asked, "Are you awake (in the everyday sense), or are you in deep sleep right now?" you'd probably say, "Awake!" If you think more deeply about it, you may be tempted to say that it's possible that you are *dreaming*, but you probably don't think you are in deep sleep at the moment. So it seems obvious that some kind of sentience is appearing. And what is it that this sentience is appearing *to*? *That* is the witnessing awareness that the nondualists talk about. The following table spells out the difference between waking-state sentience and witnessing awareness, and in Experiment 15 below, we will take a close look at whether we directly experience the brain to cause witnessing awareness.

Waking State Sentience	Witness Awareness
Is apprehended by witnessing awareness	Apprehends waking-state sentience
Comes and goes	Never comes and goes
Measured by science	Measuring and science appear to it
Appears to be an object along with other objects	Never appears or disappears; can't be an object
There is at least one per person	Never more than one, and even that is too much to say!
You are there even if it is not there	It IS you; you as awareness are never not...

These reactions, abilities and reports measure the responsiveness or sentience of an organism. Awareness is that which these phenomena appear to.

The Brain And Sentience

Neuroscience can create experimental correlations between parts of the brain and aspects of waking-state or dream-state sentience. As many inquirers have told me, "Hey, remove my brain, and that's the end of consciousness!" That may be the end of a certain span of waking-state sentience, but it cannot be the end of witnessing awareness. If removal of the brain happens, it appears to witnessing awareness, which is beyond the brain.

The very removal of the speaker's brain requires witnessing awareness to "take note" of it as an event. This is another difference between witnessing awareness and sentience. We would say that the speaker's sentience depends on the speaker's brain. But we wouldn't say that witnessing awareness, which is not personal, depends on the speaker's brain. Even the speaker depends upon witnessing awareness, but witnessing awareness doesn't depend on any speaker.

Even if all universes cease, awareness is not a kind of entity or object that can disappear along with them. It isn't an object in the first place. Awareness is THAT to which the coming and going of universes appear. Regardless of what comes and goes, awareness IS.

Experiment 15 – Does Awareness Arise From The Brain?

Purpose – Discovering whether we directly experience awareness being caused by the brain.

Objects needed – A photo or image of a brain. You can Google for brain images and use one of them displayed on your computer screen.

Setup – Sit in front of your computer so that you can see the image on screen.

The Experiment – Sit comfortably. Begin with the Heart Opener.

1 Look at the image of the brain. It arises visually as color. If you were there to feel it, it would arise tactually as texture, warmth/coolness, hardness/softness. These are all directly experienced and arise freely in open, clear awareness.

2 Do you see the color giving rise to impersonal witnessing awareness? Do you actually witness a causal process going on where the color is seen to cause witnessing awareness to appear? What would that even look like? How can the process create awareness, when awareness is already present, apprehending the process itself?

3 Do you feel a texture causing witnessing awareness to arise? Aside from the texture associated with the table, what is there additionally in direct experience that could create the existence of witnessing awareness? What would that even feel like? And isn't witnessing awareness already present in order for this creative process to appear? So how can the process create awareness?

4 Imagine that you are looking directly at a "real" brain. You may be assisting in a neurosurgical procedure. We know that in direct experience there is nothing more to a physical object than colors, tactile sensations, sounds, etc. And even these don't really "arise" since they are not separate objects in the first place. But if we are allowed to speak in terms of these visual and tactile sensations for a moment, we will check our direct experience. These sensations are arising in and appearing to sweet, open, loving witnessing awareness.

5 Do you have direct experience that these particular "brain-colors" are causing witnessing awareness? Just what would this causal process look like? Imagine that this brain were connected to an entire laboratory of scientific instruments measuring various sorts of reactivity and mentation. Let's say for a moment that you do seem to have direct experience of these processes seemingly causing awareness. What is this direct experience appearing in? Witnessing awareness is already present before the causal process even arises. So these processes cannot possibly cause the witnessing awareness that preceded it. These processes can't cause that to which they appear. It was already there!

Conclusion – It is not our experience that witnessing awareness is not present. Therefore it is not our direct experience that witnessing awareness comes into existence based on a causal process. The process itself must appear in witnessing awareness, which was there "first." Awareness is always and already.

Even though writers on nonduality and neuroscience may use the word "consciousness," they don't say the same things about it. They aren't talking about the same "thing." For this reason there is no contradiction between nonduality and neuroscience. Neuroscience measures a subtle object. This subtle object is a kind of sentience, a local reactivity associated with a biological organism. This sentience is an arising in the witnessing awareness that is your true nature, your direct experience, infinite sweetness and unconditional love.

Nonduality and neuroscience – you can think of them as different songs.

Conclusion To The Body As Container

Containers are useful objects in an everyday sense. Containment "works" as a way of speaking about beverages and petroleum products. We can even say in everyday terms that the cranium contains the brain. But as for experience itself, awareness itself, we've made the liberating discovery that containment is not an accurate metaphor. Not only is it inaccurate, but it causes a sense of alienation. Even for Descartes, who was such a passionate proponent of the container metaphor, the metaphor was associated with an exacerbated sense of separation from the world. For us, the very discovery that it's only a metaphor frees us. It frees us from mistaking an outmoded image as the literal truth of our experience. In our direct experience, there is no containment, inclusion, holding, enclosure, grasping, restriction, limitation or dominion. Experience is free, open, borderless and unlimited.

No Internal, No External

Internal and external are never our experience! Throughout this book so far, I've used the word "external" many times, mostly referring to "external objects." That was towards the beginning, to clarify the way we normally think of the world in everyday or even conventional scientific terms. But it turns out that this phrase makes no sense in direct experience.

Normally, we speak of external objects as physical things in the world that happen to be outside the body, or momentarily outside the scope of our personal perception or knowledge. The idea, of course, is that perception and awareness are limited, and that these things reside beyond those limits. Under the right circumstances, according to this view, these external objects can become "internal." This means "internal to our perception or awareness." There are two reasons that the internal/external distinction doesn't make literal sense.

One reason is that in direct experience we never experience anything "physical" or spatial in the first place. Without true, objective physicality, these essentially spatial distinctions have no literal meaning: *internal/external, inside/outside, here/there, present/absent*. Experience never confirms objects that actually have other objects inside them or outside them.

The other reason is that in direct experience we never experience containment. So not only are there no actual physical containers with stuff inside them, we can't even say that experience is one big container with some subtle things inside it and other subtle things outside it. We never experience any walls or borders to awareness and hence no "insideness" or "outsideness."

Awareness Can't Be Personal

Being free from the presumption of physicality and the metaphor of containment has also freed us from an entire cluster of limiting assumptions about ourselves and the world. Physical walls, borders and containers simply do not make sense, and do not limit anything. There is no physical separation between my true self, body and world. We have found no containment or limitation where "I" stops. If I did have a body, it would be the world.

Also, we have found no way that awareness can be contained or divided in any physical way. We have found no physical walls or borders. Physicality and its limitations are concepts, which are nothing more than (non-physical) thoughts. There is nothing stopping awareness from spilling over and being everything, which it already is!

Because awareness is not experienced as being physically divided, it cannot be personal. We have found no way in experience or even in reasonable theory that awareness can be "one per person." What would distinguish one "person's" awareness from another's? We have found no physical borders between persons either. We have not found awareness inside a person (we have not really found a "person" either). The notion of a "person" is an arising appearing in awareness.

Because awareness isn't experienced as persona, it cannot have personal characteristics. "My awareness" can't be different from "your awareness." We have found no way that awareness can even be "my awareness." Where would the owner be located? What is this "me" which would own awareness? Where is this "me" supposed to be located? Outside awareness? Underneath awareness? To the left of it? The idea that awareness is an inner core, a personal possession or an individual trait stops making sense and dissolves into freedom.

The Body: Summary Experiments

We have examined the body closely in many different ways and discovered that, wherever we look and the more closely we look, all we encounter is awareness itself.

So let's try to put all our discoveries together in some experiments that involve a fuller range of experience.

Let's add the sense of movement to the sense of positionality.

Experiment 16 – A Walk In The Park

Purpose – Discovering the direct experience of locomotion, effort, intention and sensation. Discovering whether these experiences directly establish the body as something objective that causes or contains awareness.

Objects needed – "Your" body. A park, field, beach, woods or other open space where you can walk freely. It should be a safe and peaceful place with minimal chance of meeting up with pedestrians, cars, rollerblades or bicycles. The space doesn't have to be in "nature" – even a huge empty parking lot can be used.

Setup – Before beginning to walk through this space, sit down for a moment and do the Heart Opener. YOU as witnessing awareness are the spaciousness to which arisings appear. Don't just "think" it, don't just "feel" it, but rest in its clarity. Stand as this awareness, fall in love with it.

The Experiment – Walk through this space freely at a comfortable pace, meandering any which way that presents itself.

1 There may seem to be trees, rocks, dirt, sand, water, wind, birds and other "objects." But in your direct experience, are they really objects that are separated from you the way we normally believe? Is it actually your direct experience that you are "in this location" and the tree is "in that location over there"?

2 Even if it seems that the trees and other "objects" are really arising sensations, is even this really true? Colors, sounds, aromas, warmths, coolnesses, textures, hardnesses and softnesses. Is it your direct experience that sensations are really present as objects which are being communicated to you? Do you have direct experience of sensations really being "there," waiting around for you to pick them up? Do you experience a sensation as a real object which is then given to you in experience? Do you actually experience a gap between senser and sensation? Or is there a loose, free, non-objective openness and presence to experience?

3 Notice the feeling of your "feet on the ground." Your feet and the ground are like the trees. Is the ground really there in direct experience as a part of the earth, as ground? And your feet – is it your direct experience that there are actual, objective feet? Even the feelings of hardness and resistance, even the sounds of scraping, scuffing or crunching – are these really present as objective sensations or feelings? Do you experience any of these things as being apart from awareness? Or does it seem more to be the particular and inseparable flavor of awareness?

4 Notice the feeling of your arms swinging. In the feeling of swinging, is there direct experience of an actual arm doing the swinging? In the visual impression of arms moving, is there direct visual experience of arms, in addition to color? And even the feelings and colors – are they really directly experienced to be there available to appear? How would you know that, apart from direct experience itself? Do you have direct experience of anything beyond experience?

5 Movement: Stop walking for a moment. Keep your eyes open. Turn your head to the side, first one way then the other. There may seem to be moving colors, and there may seem to be a kind of a flowing kinesthetic feeling. There might be cracking sounds (like with my "neck"!). There might even be a thought that says, "I'm moving my head." But aside from these various arisings, is there in your direct experience really a head to be experienced? Is there something solid, physical and objectively present, which is then directly experienced as moving?

6 More movement: Resume walking. As you are walking, is there direct experience that you are **really walking**? Perhaps there are more colors, kinesthetic feelings, crunching sounds, maybe aches and pains, feelings of effort or intent, or feelings and thoughts that say, "I'm tired," or "This is peaceful," or "This is boring." But is there direct experience of something truly here that is moving from one place to another? Even what may seem to be arising sensations – is it your direct experience that they are really "walking"?

7 Try to find an inclined path or stairway so that you can experience the feeling of effort from walking uphill. Ordinarily the unpleasantness of the feeling of effort, plus the possible burning sensation "in your legs," has a strong reality effect. It hurts so it seems real. Your thighs and knees, the ground and the pain all seem all too real. We usually think that if it doesn't go away when we want it to, it must be very real. But apart from the discomfort and sense of flow that we call movement, is there anything in the experience that the experience points to?

Do you directly experience an objectively existent body actually doing the moving? In this particular experiment, we have added one element that was not in previous experiments: the sense of discomfort through effort. If a truly objective body was not directly experienced without this "effort" element, then how can the mere addition of this element confer reality or independence from awareness upon the body?

Is the notion "It hurts therefore it is real" anything other than a concept or belief?

Conclusion To A Walk In The Park

If there is no direct experience that there is an objective world or body actually there doing things, then perhaps it is just possible that all this is happening in YOU as perfect clear openness, as witnessing awareness itself. (It will turn out that it is even too much to say that it is happening in any way at all. We will cover that in the section below on pure consciousness.) But for now, if you really look closely, your direct experience is not that you are a moving body in a stationary world, but that the body and world and even movingness are arising to YOU as clear, unmoving, unchanging, open, loving, witnessing awareness.

You can repeat and verify these discoveries in hundreds of different ways. Be inventive and creative about it!

PART 3 – MIND

Descartes walks into a bar. The bartender asks, "Can I get you a martini?" Descartes says, "I don't think..." and then he disappears.

The mind is usually thought of as everything about the person that is not the body.

We will discover that the mind is nothing other than awareness in the very same way we discovered that the body and world are nothing but awareness. Actually, with the realizations we have made so far, we'll find it much easier to make this discovery about the mind.

Why Is The Mind Important?

Because it seems real. It seems like it belongs to me. Or it seems to be me. It seems to be where feeling and sentience take place. It seems totally separate from other minds. And it seems perishable and impermanent.

There is also a paradox about the mind that makes it seem impossible to transcend. Some teachings that go by the name of "nondual" actually leave the inquirer at the level of a subtle mind state. They claim to arrive at witnessing awareness or pure consciousness, but only get as far as a mental state or psychological category. Often the state or category is quite pleasant. Landing in a pleasant mental state is usually a big improvement over life as it was. I have heard people say,

"I can get into pure consciousness any time I want"

or

"I was in witnessing awareness for an entire month!"

But – notice how these statements sound like the announcement of being in a certain **mood**. If a mood can come, then it can go. These cases of "being in" are instances of being in something phenomenal and therefore temporal and impermanent. If you can "get into" something, then you can also "get out" of it too.

Why Investigate The Mind?

We are investigating the mind so that we will not make this mistake. We don't want to mistake a subtle object for that clarity in which objects arise. We don't want to announce that we have "arrived" at witnessing awareness, only to be knocked out of it when the bill collector calls or we hear bad news from our doctor.

Getting Past The Mind

In principle, it's easy. It's a matter of seeing that what we believed was the **subject** and our nature (the mind) is really an arising **object**. We are really that to which the mind appears. This is the same sort of realization we have already made about the world and the body.

But when you're looking into things, the mind can be more slippery than the world or body. Where do you start? What do you do? It seems that you can't get around it in order to look at it. The mind seems to be doing the thinking. It seems to be what is "observing" everything, even our inquiry into awareness. There seems to be more in back of the mind. That stuff seems to be hidden. This actually makes the mind seem even more real and mysterious. This leads to a mysterious seeming paradox. Just as an eye can't see itself or a knife can't cut itself, it seems that the mind can't fully know itself, because that very knowing part is momentarily unobserved, so it's left out of the picture of the known. So it seems like the structure of the mind has us locked in. It seems that we can never transcend the mind, even though nondual teachings say that we *must*, in order to find freedom.

It seems that we're stuck!

But it's actually much easier than all that.

The ironic and beautifully simple discovery we'll make totally frees us from these dualistic beliefs and assumptions. We will see that in direct experience, there is nothing objective, hidden or separate about the mind whatsoever. Our only direct experience of the "mind" is awareness.

But don't we already know this about the mind, as part of Nonduality 101? "The mind is nothing but a bundle of thoughts." "Show me your mind," (and we feel sure that this is impossible). These phrases at their best embody insights that can trigger the intense realization that a mind simply cannot be found. But we may have heard them and not been shifted or transformed. These deep insights might have become just another set of beliefs or even nondual cheerleading slogans!

So what then? What do we do if these phrases **don't** do the trick? What if these nondual insights don't shake loose the ways we think about the mind? Well, in that case we might have to take a closer look and see for ourselves what's going on. We'll find out "what is my direct experience of the mind?"

In doing so, we'll see that the mind is not an objectively existing thing with its own separate, independent reality. We will see that there is no observing, thinking or processing done by the mind. We'll discover that there's nothing hidden in the mind. This is similar to the insight that we never experience an unexperienced color. We will see that the mind, like the world and the body, is nothing other than awareness itself.

Cultural Interlude

It may or may not be helpful to take a look at why we think about the mind the way we do. In the East, there are Vedantic and Buddhist notions of the mind that are quite different from the modern Western notions. You may find that when you learn that our current popular model of the mind was an invention, then you may feel greater "permission" to set it aside and follow your direct experience! If not, then you may skip down to Experiment 17.

In the West, the mind has usually been dualistically distinguished from the body, but it hasn't always been characterized as a separate, finite container. For Homer (~9th century BCE), the mind was more holistic than it was for later writers. It was different from the body, but it wasn't an essence underlying other things. It was characterized pragmatically, as a combination of character, learning, choices, behaviors and actions. For Plato (427-347 BCE), the mind was the intellect, which had access to eternal immaterial forms that existed before the objects of the world. For example, a form would be something like The Good or even A Chair, and it would exist as an extremely subtle template in a non-physical sense. In the worldly sense, a good person or a physical chair gets its identity only by being a shadow or example of the form. If someone points to a chair and asks, "What is that?" the true answer would depend on the form responsible for the chair. Forms are not sensible, but only intelligible. For this reason, the true chair cannot be known by the senses, but only by the intellect, which is also not physical. For Neoplatonists (from the 3rd century CE up to the 13th century), the mind was an eternal immaterial spark made of the same essence as The One. It could attain higher and higher levels after each succeeding rebirth, and at the state of perfection it would return to The One from which it came.

It wasn't until the 17th century that the notion of mind arose as a container of thoughts and a reflector of external reality.

A Ghost In The Machine: Alienating Metaphors

In the 17th century, the sciences of optics and mechanics were on the rise. People thought of the body as a machine, and the mind as a faculty that mirrors an outer reality as a set of inner thoughts. It's almost as though this faculty is an inner observer or a ghost in the machine. What began as speculative work by René Descartes and other writers became something we now take as the literal truth of our experience. Even in the 21st century, we're still captivated by containing and mirroring. These are harshly dualistic metaphors, cutting up experience in various ways: inside/outside, appearance/reality, knowledge/belief, self/other and more. If I believe things like the following, how can I not feel alienated from everything other than my mind?

- I'm in here.

- Reality is out there.

- My knowledge is supposed to accurately reflect reality, but it probably doesn't.

- All I can be sure of is what appears inside my mind. I might not be able to know reality.

Now let's take a closer look at how these metaphors work.

The Container Metaphor

In Part 2 we were introduced to the container metaphor, applied to the body or head as something that holds awareness in. We discovered that the containment of awareness is never our experience and that awareness is never personal. But what about the mind? Does it contain thoughts?

> *... sensory perception and imagination themselves,*
> *considered simply as mental events, certainly do occur*
> *in me.*

Meditations on First Philosophy (1641)

We say things like "I'll keep that in mind," or "I can't wrap my mind around that," or "out of sight, out of mind." If we forget or suppress something, we speak of it as being submerged, buried or blocked. We tend to take these words literally, as though the mental contents are really there, but merely hidden or located in another compartment out of view. We think of the container of the mind as holding even smaller containers, such as the conscious, subconscious, unconscious and the memory. I myself used to visualize these in spatial terms as being inside the head, inside the mind, with walls between them. We also think the mind is walled off from the outer world and from other minds. We think that there are some things on the inside of the mind, but that most things are on the outside. How can we not feel divided when we think of ourselves in this way?

The Mirror Metaphor

The human understanding is like a false mirror, which,
receiving rays irregularly, distorts and discolors the
nature of things by mingling its own nature with it.

Francis Bacon, Novum Organum (1620)

We think that the mind is a mirror of an external reality. We think that thoughts reflect and resemble this external reality. We think that the goal of knowledge is to be "accurate," which means that image and reality should match. Of course, we're not exactly sure how this happens. When we think about this mirroring that constitutes knowledge, we can't seem to put our fingers on just what the world contributes in raw material, versus what the mind does with what comes from the world. We're sure they are distinct from each other, and that they're involved. And we're sure that the resulting knowledge is an accurate reflection of the reality of the world. We're sure that thoughts mirror the world. On one side of the mirror is our image. On the other side is reality itself. Never the twain shall meet. What a perfect dualistic recipe for even more alienation!

The East Has Them Too

We can't put all the blame on Descartes and Francis Bacon. The mirror metaphor has also been found in the East, before the 17th century. The **Platform Sutra** suggests and then deconstructs the mirror metaphor. The sutra was composed around the era of Wei Lang (638-713 CE), by a famous Buddhist meditation teacher during the Chinese Tang Dynasty. It tells the story of how one day, the Fifth Ch'an Patriarch Hung-Jen asked the students to write a verse about the essence of mind. The best verse would win the place of Sixth Patriarch for the student. The local favorite, the senior student Shen-hsiu, proposed this verse:

The body is the bodhi tree,
The mind is like a clear mirror.
At all times we must strive to polish it,
And must not let the dust collect.

Then Hui-Neng, said to be an illiterate woodcutter, countered with this verse:

Bodhi originally has no tree,
The mirror(-like mind) has no stand.
Buddha-nature is always clean and pure;
Where is there room for dust to alight?

Hui-Neng "won." He became the Sixth Patriarch and is accorded as the founder of the "Sudden Enlightenment" school of Ch'an Buddhism.

What Is Our Direct Experience?

In this chapter we'll take a close look at our direct experience to check whether we actually experience the **containing** or **mirroring** functions that these metaphors suggest. We have already seen in our investigation of the world and the body that without physical objects there can't be any literal containment. There can't be mirroring either, because we found no external "reality" that can be mirrored. In this section we will discover that the "mind" itself is not the kind of object that can contain or mirror anything. We'll see how all containment and mirroring are just thoughts, and that even thoughts don't exist.

These discoveries free us from the grip of both these metaphors and the alienation that follows in their path. We will discover that everything about the "mind" is nothing other than awareness itself!

Pieces And Parts Of The Mind

We think the mind is vastly complex. But in direct experience, we'll see that it is wonderfully simple indeed. To get a handle on the complexity we believe is there, I'd like to briefly visit many different aspects of the mind that have been theorized or assumed (in the West, at least) to exist. The object is to try to experience directly that no matter what kind of aspect we attribute to the mind, the mind is never experienced as a separate, independent entity. Of course, the mind is not generally thought of as a *physical* entity, but rather a *subtle* entity of some sort. We will discover that no part of the mind is experienced as separate and independent from witnessing awareness.

To give some order to this inquiry, I'll divide coverage of the mind into different parts: objects, structures, functions and states. The idea is not to come up with an encyclopedic list with rigidly defined categories that are mutually exclusive and jointly exhaustive. Rather, the idea is to try to cover all the usual bases (even if there is some overlap), so we don't think a crucial aspect of the mind has been ignored.

When we think of the mental field as so complicated, the discovery of its utter simplicity will be even more delicious! But if you'd like, you can skip these lists and continue below, at the section called "That Sounds TIRING! What Is Our Direct Experience?"

Mental Objects

By "mental objects" I mean those things we feel arise and are seen by the mind. This would include all kinds of different thoughts, feelings, emotions, perceptions, images, realizations, intuitions, clairvoyant communications, guesses, beliefs, inferences, choices, conclusions, desires, hopes, fears, inclinations, aversions, memories, values, purposes, goals, etc. In spiritual paths, one goal can be to burn up or exhaust certain kinds of objects called *vasanas* (karmic tendencies or unconscious propensities) or *kleshas*, which can be negative objects that cloud the mind.

Mental objects are often thought to be real existents. We may identify ourselves with our memories or our values, thinking that these are the essence of what we are. We also think that there are mental objects that can be present but not currently accessible. This belief gives rise to a sense of separation "within," dividing what seems to be one part of our own self from another.

Kinds of Mental Objects

In a generic sense, we could use the term "thoughts" for all the mental objects in the list above. Many nondual teachings do just that — they call everything a "thought." But thoughts belong to minds. We will need to investigate the mind and its thoughts. Without a "mind" can there really be "thoughts"? Without "thoughts" can there really be a "mind"? We will look into these issues quite thoroughly. After examining the mind, we'll see that using the word "thought" as a common denominator for certain kinds of objects still carries the psychological traces and implications of "mind." If we are seeking to know our true self, but remain limited by the notion of an individual mind, we will continue to feel separated. We will feel separated from (what we imagine to be) "other minds" and from (what we visualize as) the "world outside the mind" as well. Our experiential investigation of the mind will actually burst the notion of this individual mind-bubble with its limiting assumptions.

We will take a look at many of the types of objects in the list, such as thoughts, emotions, memories, etc., beginning with those objects that have the most to do with our suffering.

Suffering

Suffering is related to believing our thoughts. In fact, some teachings even define suffering as the objection to pain and unpleasantness. They say, "Pain is inevitable; suffering is optional." In such a case, suffering is possible only because we believe our thoughts about the situation and about how the pain shouldn't exist. Without believing any of our thoughts, we would never suffer. We might experience aches and pains, but never be suffering.

Here are some examples of thoughts that can be believed. Of course, not every thought causes suffering in every case. But the belief component is always there.

- "I not am enlightened."

- "The Dow will probably rise next quarter."

- "2+2=4."

- "I'm the only one in my family who went to college."

- "I understand why I got the promotion."

- "Dzogchen Buddhism is the most effective path."

- "There is special energy in Arunachala that will get me enlightened if my boss would only give me enough vacation time to travel there."

- "We can't change the fact that I'm still a person."

- "No one likes me."

- "Other people are better than I am."

- "It's not fair that I should have to die so soon."

- "I am enlightened."

Some forms of psychological therapy specialize in reducing the number and intensity of negative thoughts about ourselves. Other methods work on lessening the degree of belief in thoughts that do come up. The prevalence of these forms of therapy attests to the power that thoughts have over us when we believe them.

But these methods don't question the very notions of thought and belief. So they end up leaving in place the dualistic structures involving thought/reality, truth/falsity and belief/disbelief. The presence of these structures in turn allows for the possibility of future suffering.

But what if we could be free of the structures themselves? In direct experience we will see that none of these structures can be found.

The Structure Of Thought

For most of us in the modern West, thought is given structure by a network of assumptions involving knowledge and the world. There are many ways to think about thought and belief. But in my own case, for much of my life my assumptions followed the "Realist" models of the world discussed in Part 1. I was convinced that thought at its best represents or mirrors a state of affairs in the world. Much of my own nondual inquiry consisted of examining this very conviction. And after spending many years helping other people with these issues, I began to realize that I was not alone in being a Realist. For most people, pretty much the same assumptions are operative:

- Truth and reality exist outside of thought. They are what they are and don't depend on thought.

- Thoughts are supposed to mirror reality, but they can also get reality wrong.

- Thoughts usually express a proposition or meaning or something that is either true or false. Truth means an accurate mirroring of reality; falsehood is an inaccurate mirroring. We may not always know the truth value of a given proposition. We can feel strongly about the truth of something whether we are sure or not.

- Thoughts can be believed or disbelieved.

- Belief means a commitment to the truth of what the thought expresses. When we believe a thought, we think the thought mirrors reality accurately. When we disbelieve a thought, we think it doesn't mirror reality accurately.

- One needn't believe or disbelieve a thought. One may also be uncommitted or neutral towards a thought, not having a view or caring about what the thought expresses.

The Collapse Of Structure

In Parts 1 and 2, we made several crucial and liberating discoveries that totally dismantle the "Realist" structure of thought. We can be free from the structures of thought and their attendant beliefs. And this allows us to become free from thought itself. Let's take the following thought as an example to work with:

(A) There is a fresh orange on the table in front of me.

We think (A) is true if it accurately mirrors reality. That is, (A) is true if there is **really** a red apple, **really** a table, **really** a me, etc. But we looked and in direct experience didn't find anything of the kind! All we found was awareness.

Let's try it again!

Experiment 17 – Thinking About An Orange

Purpose – Discovering whether direct experience establishes that thought has a direct object.

Objects needed – A table or desk. A chair. A fresh orange.

Setup – As with the earlier exercise with the orange, find a fresh orange with a bright, uniform color. Clear a place on the table so that the orange can have a few inches of clear space around it. Place the orange in the center of that space.

The Experiment – Sit in front of the table so that you are able to see the orange clearly. Begin with the Heart Opener so that you get a taste of being the open clear spaciousness of awareness.

1 Look at the orange openly and intently as though you had to memorize what it looks like.

2 Close your eyes and visualize the orange as vividly as you can.

3 (Eyes still closed.) Allow the following thought (A) to arise.

(A) "There is a fresh orange on the table in front of me."

You may also say it out loud or imagine it written down. Try to believe it as strongly as you can:

4 (Eyes still closed.) Try to imagine what would make (A) true. It usually seems that (A) would be true if there really is an orange on the table in front of you! Imagine how you would test for the truth of (A). We will use a very good test: direct experience.

5 Open your eyes. Now test for the truth of (A). Look and touch and taste all you want. In direct experience, is there really an orange there? If you worked your way through Part 1, you may remember how we explored our direct experience in order to discover the truth of what's going on. If this is a little obscure or difficult, you may revisit Part 1, especially Experiments 1 – 5.

- Apart from the sensations of color, texture and flavor, do you directly experience an orange itself? Can you experience the orange in the absence of these things? (No.)

- Apart from vision, do you directly experience a color? Can you directly experience color in the absence of vision? (No.)

- Apart from the tactile sense, do you directly experience a texture? (No.)

- Apart from the sense of gustation, do you directly experience a flavor? (No.)

- Apart from witnessing awareness, do you directly experience the visual, tactile or gustatory sense? (No.)

- Apart from witnessing awareness, what do you experience as being really present to be experienced? When you think about the orange is the orange really present, waiting for you to experience it? When you think about an orange color, is the color present and waiting for you? Can you even tell whether you are apprehending the color or creating it?

- If you were using a microscope and even a lab full of scientific instruments, do you think the end result would be any different? Sooner or later, all scientific instruments result in some kind of perception, such as marks on a screen or a page or a dial, which are basically just more colors. So the case of having scientific instruments becomes parallel to the case of not having instruments.

- Do you directly experience the orange to be on the table?

With no actual orange, (A) can't be true. But is (A) false? Let's negate (A) and see if the negation is true. If the negation of (A) is really true, then (A) is really false:

(A1) "**It is not the case that** there is a fresh orange on the table in front of me."

This one is not much better. It implies that there is a table there, but no orange. But in our direct experience we have already examined physical objects, including the body. We have never found anything to really be present to be perceived. Physical objects were nothing more than perceptions, which were nothing more than perceiving, which was nothing more than witnessing awareness itself. We never found any true physical objects. So in the case of (A1), how can there be a table? How can there be a "me" or a "front"? We have looked and have never found any of these things!

Review Of Experiment 17

To be sure, (A) is a very concrete thought. Very few thoughts seem easier to test, to investigate, to verify. But we have seen that we can't find anything in direct experience that matches or mirrors (A). It's not that (A) is false. There is no experience of an orange or a table, so it doesn't make sense to attribute truth or falsity to (A). Rather, (A) is not our experience. We are freed from believing (A). We are also free from disbelieving (A). We are free from the structure of assumptions that make (A) seem as if it requires a belief-kind of attitude.

We have seen how we can be freed of the belief in thoughts like (A). This discovery keeps us open to many wonderful possibilities. We can be open to the arising of brilliant orange colors and tasty sensations (as though we were "really eating the orange") without the necessity of believing that the orange really exists, and also without believing that it is somehow "missing." We are free from both sides of the duality, "existence" as well as "non-existence."

To Do On Your Own

You can try this kind of experiment on almost any thought that seems interesting. It might be easier on thoughts we feel neutral about. Try these first, then gradually try thoughts that may be more charged for you.

In this investigation, we are not trying to stamp out thought or falsify it. We are looking deeply into the structure of thought; we're seeing that truth and falsity conditions can never be met in direct experience.

What about thoughts that are not so concrete and don't seem to depend on physicality and perception? What about a purely conceptual thought?

Experiment 18 – A Purely Conceptual Thought

Purpose – Discovering whether a conceptual thought represents anything objective.

Objects needed – A table or desk. A chair. A pen. A piece of paper. Four matchsticks or paperclips.

Setup – Sit at the table. Place the pen and paper in front of you. Arrange the four matchsticks or paperclips in front of you.

The Experiment – Begin with the Heart Opener so that you get a taste of being the open clear spaciousness of awareness.

1 Our "conceptual thought" will be an abstract one.

(B) "2+2=4."

2 Get a good "feel" for this thought. Write down the numbers on the piece of paper. Perform addition as you would in grade-school arithmetic class. Play with the matchsticks. Put two of them in front of you, then count them. Add two more. Count those. Then count the total number of matchsticks.

3 Get a good "feel" – what does it feel like to believe this thought? Try to make the belief strong.

4 Imagine as vividly as you can just how you would test this belief. Remember that belief is the commitment to the truth behind the thought. When we think a thought points to something true, we most often think that there is some accurate mirroring going on somehow. There is a long history in which mathematics is regarded as being written into nature beyond thought.

> *The laws of nature are but the*
> *mathematical thoughts of God.*

Euclid (330-260 BCE)

5 Let's test it in direct experience. What is mirrored in the case of thought (B)? I'll suggest some ways you may try to verify the truth of this thought.

- It seems like thoughts, when pointing to the truth, must mirror a reality outside of thought. Well, then – just what does "2+2=4" mirror?

- Does the column of numbers written on your piece of paper verify the thought? But wait! Are they really numbers, or do they disappear into witnessing awareness the same way the orange did?

- Can you approach the verification by using a calculator? You press the "2" key, then the "+" key, then the "2" key again. Then you press the "=" key. In the display you see a "4" appear.

  But wait! What really happened in direct experience? The actions are experienced as movements, which are experienced as flows in the kinesthetic sense and textures and hardnesses in the tactile sense. The numbers in the display are experienced as colors. We're back to the same situation we encountered with the orange, where in direct experience, objects disappeared into sensations, sensations disappeared into sensing, and sensing – into witnessing awareness. There are no keys or numbers directly experienced as being there. There's no calculator there. There's no action of pressing there. In fact, there's no "there" there!

  Is there a wholly conceptual realm where these thoughts abide? If so, what is it, where is it? Apart from the thoughts, inscriptions of numbers, and presses of the calculator keys, can you find this realm?

  You can repeat this particular attempted method of verification by thinking about all the math classes you've had and all the math books you've worked with. You can even add all the Google searches and websites you can find. Do they establish any conceptual or abstract truth to exist beyond the realm of thought? There might be an arising that says, "This really fits logically with all the math I know." But based on that arising (and any others), how do you establish the existence of an abstract truth that is pre-existent and actually discovered by thought? We think that axioms and logical laws actually govern thought and truth, but where are these laws to be found? Where do they reside?

■ Can you prove that thought (B) ("2+2=4") is true by proving **other** thoughts and then using them in support of **this** one? Don't use any physical objects; just think about it. Try it. Here is an example of how a proof might go.

"Proof" (BP)
(a) "1+1+1+1 = 4."
(b) "OK, I see."
(c) "1+1+1+1 = 2+2."
(d) "So far, so good. We're getting there."
(e) "Equal numbers are equal to each other."
(f) "Therefore, because of (a) – (e): 2+2=4."
(g) "(B) is true."
(h) "Yay!"

But wait! In trying to show that a purely conceptual thought (B) can be true, we used several other conceptual thoughts in a sequence, (a) – (g). How does this series of thoughts prove that (B) is true? Did we at any point directly experience a matchup between (B) and a reality outside of thought? We can ask the same question about each of the other thoughts in the series. What makes each of them true? Nothing in series of thoughts in "Proof (BP)" allowed us to escape the realm of thought. We haven't experienced any mirroring and cannot prove that mirroring takes place.

- OK, let's assume we did find a link between (a) – (g) and (B). Now we have a compressed version of Proof (BP):

"Proof" (BP1)
"(a) – (g) logically prove (B), so 2+2=4."

But wait! (BP1) is itself merely another thought. We are still not outside the realm of thought. We haven't burst through to a reality beyond thought. We have yet to find a case in which a thought can establish in direct experience the truth of another thought.

- How about a deep feeling of certainty? Does that prove (B)?

"Proof" (BP2)
(a) "I feel the truth of (B) deeply in my bones, without a doubt."
(b) "Therefore (B) must be true."

Well, (BP2) doesn't establish the truth of (B) either, and for two reasons. One reason is that even in the everyday sense, we all know that a feeling of certainty is an unreliable guide to truth. The second and more important reason is this. (BP2) doesn't prove anything as far as direct experience goes. (BP2) is merely another series of thoughts that isn't any different from the other series (BP1) and (BP). We have yet to directly experience any mirroring.

Review Of Experiment 18

In this experiment, (B) is a conceptual, abstract thought. Because it belongs to the subject of mathematics, we're used to thinking that it mirrors something perhaps very subtle and profound. But we were unable to directly experience any mirroring. We never experienced anything the thought points to.

Notice the irony here that "mirroring" is a physical metaphor. The metaphor refers to material objects and their likenesses reflected in polished surfaces. In the everyday sense of mirroring, it works fine. We're able to verify the likeness against the original. We can look at the object and also at its image in the mirror and compare them to each other.

But the metaphor totally breaks down when applied to thought itself. It can't help us verify the truth of thought against a reality outside of thought. There is simply no "non-thought" that we can compare a thought to, visually or in any other way.

The best we can do is evaluate a thought against another thought. In fact, this is what all of our "proofs" did. But it doesn't get us anywhere in showing how the first thought corresponds to reality. The second thought is a thought just like the first one is. In fact, the entire process of evaluation is also just a series of thoughts. None of these thoughts can bootstrap our experience outside of the realm of thought into a reality beyond thought.

Thoughts Have No Binary Truth Value

In the same way we have no direct experience of the **truth** of a conceptual thought, we have no direct experience of the **falsity** of a conceptual thought. (B) is not false either. That is, it doesn't mirror a reality outside of thought in an inaccurate way. Why not? Because in direct experience there is simply no mirroring to be found. Neither accurate mirroring nor inaccurate mirroring. (B) doesn't hit the mark. And it doesn't miss the mark. There is no mark.

But Thought Is Made Of Truth

There is a deeply profound way in which *all* thought is true. *A thought is made out of truth*, the truth of your experience and your nature as awareness. When we look deeply into the objects or referents mentioned in a thought, there is nothing separate that we observe. Nothing separate is experienced to be present. Our only experience is awareness itself. The thought is actually this awareness itself, which is the truth of our experience.

Another way to look at the truth of thought is this. A thought arises from the background of awareness. It subsists or stands in awareness as awareness. And it subsides back into awareness. Any thought returns to its true home, which is awareness. This is how it unerringly points to the truth. This can be verified in direct experience at any moment with any thought. It works not only for the "I-thought," but for **any** thought!

Thoughts Have No Referents

There are no objects or referents of thought. A thought of an orange doesn't point to a real orange. A thought of "2+2=4" doesn't point to a heavenly equation in God's mind. Despite the nondual cliché that "Thoughts are just pointers," we never experience a thought pointing to anything.

It might seem that thoughts point. Let's look more closely. Let's say you have several thoughts in a row:

1 (Thought "A") "There is an orange on the table."

2 (Thought "B") [Orange color]

3 (Thought "C") [Sweet, tangy flavor]

3 (Thought "D") [Sweet, citric-like aroma]

4 (Thought "E") "Thought 'A' did not point to a real orange, but to thoughts 'B', 'C' and 'D'."

There is nothing thought points to. When thought "A" is on the scene supposedly doing its pointing, thoughts "B," "C," and "D" haven't yet arisen to be pointed to. And when "B," "C," and "D" each arise, the "pointing" thought "A" is no longer there.

When a thought arises that says, "A points to B," this is just a thought *about* pointing. It doesn't actually indicate any pointing. There is never any true pointing outside of a thought that claims it.

Actually, the only place to which all thoughts "point" is awareness. They do this by subsiding back into awareness. This is how they "point." This is our direct experience.

Thought Exercises To Do On Your Own

You can try this kind of experiment with any conceptual thought, or any thought at all. In general, you could proceed like this:

1 Try out the thought. Go for one that seems convenient for you to verify as true. No need to travel to verify thoughts about the Great Wall of China!

2 Get a good sense of what it feels like to strongly believe that the thought is true.

3 Check for what it would require to make that thought true. What are the truth conditions? How could you test and verify this thought? Do you have a kind of mirroring situation in mind, where the thought mirrors, matches or corresponds to a reality outside of thought? If not, then what do you mean when you believe that the thought is true?

4 Try to verify the thought in direct experience.

5 Then do some checking: the thought makes a claim about some "thing" or state of affairs. In doing so, it must point to certain referents and maybe background situations. Then remember what it takes to mirror or to indicate. Do you directly experience these mirrored referents and conditions as separate, independent things, or do they simply collapse into awareness?

6 If you **do** experience the collapse, then what sense does it make that the thought can actually be "true" or "false"? And if you **do** not experience the collapse, is it because you have actually found the referent as a truly existent object? In that case, just what is the reality of the separate object that you seem to be experiencing? Do you experience that separate object to exist apart from awareness?

If you **don't** experience the object to be separate from awareness, then this is the collapse. The object really isn't the "object" but awareness anyway! And if you do seem to experience the object to be separate from awareness, then it's too late. By being experienced, the object is already awareness! Realizing this is the collapse that I am talking about.

About Belief

We know what it is for a thought to arise. But what is it to *believe* a thought? What's going on there?

Normally speaking, belief is an attitude we have towards a thought, statement or proposition. It's not the thought itself, but something we think or feel about it. Schematically, it's like this:

1 (Thought "A") "My spiritual path is the most effective one."

2 (Thought "B") "I feel strongly that A is true."

   In this case, the belief about thought "A" is actually thought "B." This is ironic! When we believe a thought, it's just another thought, with maybe a touch of hope or fear (feelings) that it is true. Of course, the "believing" thought could take a different form. Instead of the mere statement that "I think 'A' is true," the believing thought could be one or more other thoughts:

3 (Thought "C") "When someone agrees with 'A', I feel a warm sense of pleasure."

4 (Thought "D") "When someone disagrees with 'A', I get hurt, angry or confused."

5 (Thought "E") "Because of 'C' and 'D', I realize that I must really believe that 'A' is true."

All of these are separate thoughts. Even the feelings and reactions mentioned in "C" and "D" are nothing more than other mental objects, other "thoughts" in a wider sense.

So the beliefs about thoughts are merely thoughts. They aren't really different from the thoughts themselves. They all arise to you, to your nature as global background witnessing awareness!

Because of what we'll discover about memory in the next exercise, it turns out that the believing thought and the believed thought are never present at the same time. They are separate and independent from each other. So belief is a claim never borne out by direct experience.

About Memory Thoughts

What about memory? Belief and memory go together pretty closely. When we believe a thought or a statement, we think the object of our belief really, truly exists. But do we directly experience that existence? Believing memory can make us feel alienated from the past, as well as attached to the past. An example of alienation from the past through memory might be remembering an insult or injury from early in life, and it can make one develop a sort of dissociative disconnection from that period of life, that period of time, or that area of the country. An example of attachment through memory might be remembering a peak spiritual experience you had, which can be accompanied by (i) a feeling that there was enlightenment back then which was subsequently lost, (ii) a feeling of intolerance for present experiences because they don't measure up by comparison, and (iii) a yearning to recapture that previous experience. In fact, unverified assumptions about memory are actually built into much of our thought.

For example, notice again the series of thoughts (A) through (E):

1 (Thought "A") "My spiritual path is the most effective one."

2 (Thought "B") "I feel strongly like 'A' is true."

3 (Thought "C") "When someone agrees with 'A,' I feel a warm sense of pleasure."

4 (Thought "D") "When someone disagrees with 'A', I get hurt, angry or confused."

5 (Thought "E") "Because of 'C' and 'D,' I realize that I must really believe that 'A' is true."

They seem simple enough. But notice that most of these thoughts refer to earlier thoughts in the series. Later thoughts refer to earlier thoughts which are no longer present. Is this reference something verifiable, or is it merely imagined as another thought? From the perspective of thought "E" which seems to point outside itself, where actually are thoughts "A" – "D"?

Is the assumption of memory borne out by our direct experience?
Let's take a look.

Experiment 19 – Remembering Breakfast

Purpose – Discovering whether memory gives you direct experience of anything in the past.

Objects needed – A chair.

Setup – Sit quietly in the chair.

The Experiment – Begin with the Heart Opener.

1 Take a few moments to remember as vividly as you can the experience of eating breakfast earlier in the day. It helps to be specific – remember the feelings of hunger and anticipation. Remember the flavors, textures, aromas, the feelings of hardness, softness, crispiness, crunchiness, moistness, dryness, spiciness, saltiness and sweetness of the food. If you haven't washed the dishes yet, you may even look at the remnants of the food on the plate and cup and knife and fork. Can you feel the food in your stomach? These things may help make the memories more vivid.

2 Now check for a moment – there seems to be a series of "memory-thoughts" occurring right now in direct experience. These present memory-thoughts seem to be recalling or referring to "breakfast thoughts" which occurred earlier when you had breakfast and experienced the thoughts originally.

3 Ask yourself how reference can actually happen. In your direct experience, how does a present memory-thought actually refer to a breakfast-thought? What is the proof that the breakfast-thought actually occurred?

▪ When the breakfast-thoughts arose, was there a memory-thought among them taking notes?

• And now, while the memory-thoughts are arising, are there any original breakfast-thoughts present to serve as the referents?

Review Of Experiment 19

We have come to a mildly shocking realization. In the same way that thoughts about oranges or "2+2" have no referents, memory thoughts have no reference.

The original thought and the later memory-thought are never present at the same time. According to the assumption that thoughts happen in a series and can refer to each other, we have made some radical discoveries:

• When the original thought is present, the memory-thought is not yet present.

• When the memory-thought arises, the original thought is long gone.

• A thought and "its" memory-thought are never co-present. They never meet and are never present together to refer or be referred to. We never directly experience reference or pointing.

• Other than a present thought that makes the claim, there is absolutely no substantiation that a previous thought ever arose. But there is no reaching out of this present thought to verify this claim.

• There is no verification for memory. "Memory" is nothing more than a current thought arising in YOU as witnessing awareness!

Memory Experiments To Do On Your Own

You can do this kind of experiment on almost anything it seems you can remember. You can examine memories of your childhood or adolescence. You can examine memories of last night's dinner. You can try pleasant or unpleasant experiences. You can try travels, sporting events, movies, meditations or any other aspect of life.

For example, let's say you had a bicycle accident and you now have a scar on your leg. The present memories, the visual and tactile sensations of the scar, the feelings of stiffness – all these are good evidence in the everyday sense that there was a previous accident. But in your direct experience, are the original thoughts currently arising? Are they allowing themselves to be pointed to by the memory-thoughts, or do you merely experience memory-thoughts that seem to point to the original thoughts?

In the everyday sense of getting around in the world as a person among other persons, we use present clues and traces and evidence to substantiate claims about the past. When you show the waiter the check where she overcharged you for a large salad instead of the small salad, she will suddenly realize, "Oh, yes! I remember, you **did** order the small!" The various cues (like the small plate in front of you) will help.

This is all fine. Nondual inquiry is open to the everyday sense of things arising as an infinitely rich multiplicity, as a flavor of awareness. But that doesn't mean that we need to *believe* the literality and objectivity of the everyday sense. We can use everyday language in a kind of knowing, pragmatic, ironic way, yet we don't need to regard the everyday sense of things, with its dualistic and often alienating assumptions, as the literal truth of our experience. Nondual inquiry frees us from this.

What About The Other Mental Objects?

We just talked a lot about "thoughts," which are the kind of mental objects that ordinarily seem like they can be true or false, and which seem like they can successfully refer to things. We found out that "thoughts" don't really have these properties.

But what about all the other mental objects, such as feelings, emotions, perceptions, images, sensations, intuitions, choices, desires, hopes, fears, inclinations, aversions, memories, values, purposes and goals?

These seem to be very different kinds of objects. The difference between them seems quite **real**. If these things are really different, then they must also be real. The yearning of a desire or the gut-wrenching anguish of fear seem so different from the mild occurrence of a tickle or a thought about "2+2=4."

Let's test this out with another experiment. Let's try to find the difference between a sensation, a thought and a feeling.

Experiment 20 – Finding The Difference Between Mental Objects

Purpose – Discovering whether we directly experience any objective difference between various "types" of mental objects. Do we directly experience "thoughts" vs. "feelings" vs. "sensations"? We think that our various experiences are different because they seem to refer to very different objects in the physical or mental world. A color seems more different from a sound and less different from another color. These differences seem real. The experiences seem to be caused by the objects, and in turn seem to refer to those objects. But what actually makes something a "color" vs. a "thought" vs. a "feeling"? We don't directly experience the object that these items seem to refer to, so what makes them seem different? The fact that they seem different adds to their reality effect. What do we encounter in direct experience?

Objects needed – A chair.

Setup – Sit quietly in the chair.

The Experiment – Begin with the Heart Opener.

1 **Sensation**: Look at the wall in front of you. Try to find a spot where the color is a simple monotone. You have already discovered that what is directly experienced is not a "wall" but an arising of vision or color in awareness. Let the color arise and abide for a while....

2 Allow the arising of color to subside.

3 **Thought**: Allow the thought to arise, "Paris is in France." If it helps, remember how you were told about this in school or at home. You might have seen the city Paris depicted on a map as a patch of color located inside another color representing the country France. Try to make this thought vivid. "Paris is in France." Allow it to abide for a while....

4 Allow the thought to subside.

5 **Feeling**: Imagine the feeling you'd get if you just found out that you received a huge inheritance from a long-lost rich aunt, and you'll be getting **one-million dollars per month for the rest of your life!** (Non-U.S. countries, consult www.xe.com for conversions.) You just opened the envelope and saw your first check. $1,000,000.00! Allow it to become vivid. What is your feeling? Surprise? Doubt? Shock? Disbelief? Disapproval? Elation? Excitement? Whatever the feeling, allow it to arise and abide for a while.

6 Allow the feeling to subside.

Inquiry – You have experienced three cases of a mental object. Officially, they are called "sensation," "thought," and "feeling." If you look back casually at the experiment, the objects seem very different from each other. But are they really different? What is your direct experience?

■ **During the sensation** – Did you directly experience the color as being different from a thought or a feeling? Was that "difference" part of your direct experience at the time? Did you directly experience anything about the color sensation that makes it different from thoughts and feelings? Did you directly experience the color coming from what is often called the "outside world"? Most likely, you'll report that none of these things happened. Instead, while the color was perceived, there was simply no direct experience of "difference from a thought or feeling." In other words, during the sensation, there was no direct experience of difference. It was experienced without a label.

■ **During the thought** – The same thing applies here too. While the thought "Paris is in France" was abiding, there was no direct experience of "difference from a sensation and feeling." There was no direct experience of a special source of the thought. It was just an arising in awareness. In fact, at the time, it wasn't even directly experienced as a thought.

■ **During the feeling** – The same applies here as well. During the thrill or confusion (or whatever) you felt by imagining getting the inheritance, there was no direct experience of "feeling is different from sensation and thought." There was no direct experience of difference and no direct experience self-labeled as "feeling."

■ **"But they seem so different NOW"** – They certainly might seem different now. Sensation. Thought. Feeling. They must be different. Right? But notice what is happening. There is a present thought that claims to look back at previous experiences and evaluate them. For example, there may be several experiences in a row:

E1: Sensation of color

E2: Thought of Paris

E3: Feeling of excitement

E4 (Which is a thought): "E1, E2 and E3 are different kinds of mental objects."

Notice that the only "difference" that arises is simply a claim made inside E4. E4 is just a thought and can't reach an object.

Conclusion To "Finding The Difference"

We see that "difference" is never directly experienced, but only claimed by the present thought. And as we have already seen, thoughts have no true objective referents. There is no place for the present thought to point other than to awareness.

Not only is there no direct experience of difference, but there is no direct experience of E1 being a sensation, E2 being a thought or E3 being a feeling. All these are simply claims made by thoughts which cannot refer to objects. The entire structure is a set-up constructed by the present thought.

It is beginning to look as if there are no differences between mental objects at all. In fact, after the next experiment, I will dispense with the everyday terms for these objects and call them all "arisings."

Two Experiences At The Same Time?

While writing this book, I received a very perceptive question by e-mail. The writer had read my book **Standing as Awareness** and was trying to do the experiments that are sketched therein. At one point he hit a roadblock. He asked, "What about various objects arising **simultane-ously**? I see two colors arising, not just one. Doesn't that prove they must be real?" What seems to be an even clearer case of simultaneous experiences, and one which poses a greater challenge for nondual investigation, is this one, "Can't I *see* the desk and *touch* the desk at the same time?" Even from some of the experiments in this book, it seems like that might be possible. For example, in the perceptual experiments I recommend focusing on only one sense, and doing the other senses at another time. This makes it seem as though the other sensations really *do* arise simultaneously and need to be blocked off. It can seem that we can block them if we want, but they're really out there pushing their way in.

So I can see the writer's point. Many nondual teachings say that only one thought or arising can happen at once. Never more than one at a time. The teachings seem to be quite certain about this. When pressed to defend the no-simultaneity thesis, nondual teachings sometimes try to explain away our impressions of simultaneity by claiming that experiences really do happen one-at-a-time, but occur subliminally much faster than we realize. The speed could be up to 40-50 per second or faster, it is sometimes said. We just don't notice it. These teachings would explain that my e-mail correspondent experienced actually red-blue-red-blue-red-blue many times very close together. He then came up with the mistaken judgment that red and blue were simultaneous when in reality they were successive and one-at-a-time.

Notice that "faster than we realize" teaching has to assume that there are mental objects that we are not aware of. For every object we are aware of, says this teaching, there are many that go by unnoticed.

Hmm, but what is a thought that I am not aware of? A thought that I am not aware of is impossible to verify through direct experience. It doesn't even make sense. Where would that thought **be** if not in awareness? And how can the person making the "faster than we realize" claim know that it is true? We are free not to entertain this "faster than we realize" claim. It will turn out that we don't need it.

Nevertheless, it seems like we should be able to get an answer to the question of whether there can be more than one experience at a time. It certainly seems like there can be at least two things arising at once. The example of **seeing** the desk and **touching** the desk at the same time is a very good one. In the everyday sense, it certainly seems that a color can arise at the same time as a texture. What's wrong with this? Can't it be true?

Part of the reason that color and texture seem to be able to arise at the same time is that it seems like they are coming from two separate sensory channels. And it seems that these channels should be able to flow simultaneously just like electricity in wires.

There is another reason we think we can have multiple experiences simultaneously: we model experiences on things. And we believe that many things exist at the same time.

Background

We will do an experiment to try to verify what happens in experience, but for now, here is a little background.

We grow up in modern Western culture influenced by the realist model of experience (see Part 1 beginning at "Naïve Realism"). I certainly was influenced by it. In fact, in my twenties, I was a young, fervent and dogmatic follower of Ayn Rand's Objectivism, which strongly asserts real, objective existence. Rand is the writer quoted at the beginning of Part 1 who wrote, "The universe exists independent of consciousness (of any consciousness)," and "Things are what they are ... they possess a specific nature, an identity."

From realism, we take it for granted that our experiences mirror things in the world. According to the realist model, there is an unlimited number of things existing in the world at any one time. Most of these things are beyond the range of experience of any single person, but there are still many mild and intense experiences happening at any one time, according to realism.

Let's take the example of my simple train ride to work. Here is a very short list of things that I seem to experience according to realism. However many things come into the scope of my experience, there are supposedly even more things unexperienced by me.

I seem to be aware of:

- The noise and motion of the car rumbling, clattering and jittering over the tracks.

- The many different people in the car with me, some reading the paper, some listening to their electronic devices (I am aware of many devices too), and some people trying to squeeze in a few more minutes of sleep before work.

- The walls of the car, maybe metallic or plastic, maybe covered with advertisements for beverages, schools, doctors, lawyers, TV shows, train schedule changes, etc.

- The many things you see outside the train windows, perhaps including the sky, the sun, the clouds, millions of raindrops, trees, bushes, houses, cars, people, lamp posts, traffic signals and more.

- The ventilation system (or lack thereof), and the temperature, movement and staleness of the air.

Even in a one-minute period of time it seems that there must be millions of things that you experience. According to the realist model of experience, our experiences mirror these things in the world. Since there are lots of things in the world at the same time, there must be lots of incoming experiences happening at the same time. How does mirroring happen? The "mirror" metaphor is based on a group of interlocking realist claims:

1 There are many things existing in the world at any one time.

2 Things in the world cause my experiences.

3 My experiences resemble things in the world.

4 I have many experiences at one time.

These claims hang together in a mutually reinforcing web. Even though we saw in Part 1 that there is no support for (1), (2) and (3), they are still given strength by (4). And we feel sure of (4) because of the power that (1), (2) and (3) still have for us. If we see that there is no direct experiential support for (4), then all of these claims will lose power over us, and we will be emancipated from the various anxieties brought on by realism.

So let's take a close look at (4) to see whether it is verified by direct experience. Let's examine an example:

4.1 A color and a texture both arise at the same time T.

This is true only if both of the following are true:

4.1a A color arises at time T.
4.1b A texture arises at time T.

Let's assume for a moment that an arising actually does arise at time T. What makes this arising a *color*? Normally we say that something is a color because we associate it with the eyes and with the modality of vision.

But by this point in our inquiry, we have already examined the world and the body. We have already realized that there is no direct experience of any object in the world. We have realized that there is no direct experience of color apart from seeing, and no direct experience of seeing apart from witnessing awareness. There simply is no experience of a color as something separate that arises. Of course, there may seem to be a thought at time T1 that claims, "That arising at time T was a color." But the thought that arises at T1 has no access to anything outside itself. It cannot verify its own claim, and another thought cannot verify it either. There is simply nothing that establishes that what arose at time T was actually a *color*.

And it is the same for the *texture*. Other than the claim of a subsequent thought, there is nothing to verify that what arose at time T was actually a *texture*.

Let's say there is an experience that seems to be of two things happening at the same time. How can we tell what is actually happening? That is, how can we tell if this experience is actually *two objects* at time

T, or *one object* at time T that *says there are two*? If there are really two simultaneous objects, they can both arise only if they are actually there to arise. Of course, we are used to suspecting that these objects must be something definite in themselves (apart from the experience "of" them). But as we have seen many times so far, this is just the old realist view again. In direct experience, there is no "of." The realist view is impossible to verify even in principle. We have no idea about how verification would even work.

The realist view turns out to be incoherent. We are not bound by this view. It doesn't accord with our direct experience. In actual direct experience, we never jump outside of experience to verify anything about "experienced objects." Nothing like that ever happens. We have no direct evidence that there were *two* objects at time T. We have no experience that the objects were present, or different from each other. In fact, we have no experience that there was *one* object either. When we see that in direct experience it is neither two nor one, then object-hood itself makes less and less sense as a model for experience. We simply don't need objects (or views about objects) in order to be, and to be happy. There is sweet and beautiful simplicity in this direct experience.

Even if it seems like the entire *universe of things* arose separately at time T, there is nothing in direct experience to substantiate this claim. We can't say that the universe is anything other than the present thought making a claim about time T. And even the "present thought" can't be verified!

So we have no direct evidential support for (4.1a) or (4.1b):

4.1a A color arises at time T.
4.1b A texture arises at time T.

So we have no direct evidential support for (4.1):

4.1 A color and a texture both arise at the same time T.

This means that the most reasonable possibility for (4),

4 I have many experiences at one time,
is also not supported. The realist web consisting of (1) "There are

many things existing in the world at any one time," (2) "Things in the world cause my experiences," (3) "My experiences resemble things in the world," and (4) "I have many experiences at one time" has lost support for its final claim.

Mental Objects: Summary Experiment

Maybe mental objects don't even arise at all! We will examine that possibility below. But before that, let's actually do an experiment to try to verify experientially the simultaneous arising of mental objects. That is, let's examine whether it is our direct experience that mental objects truly occur more than one at a time.

Experiment 21 – Fireworks

Purpose – Discovering whether we directly experience mental objects to arise simultaneously.

Objects needed – A chair.

Setup – Sit quietly in the chair.

The Experiment – Begin with the Heart Opener.

1 **Imagine this scene as vividly as possible:** You are on holiday by the seaside. You're somewhere warm, safe and sunny, with blue skies and turquoise waters. This evening, you're sitting on the deck of a café overlooking the harbor, sipping coffee and watching the sunset. The local-grown coffee has a mellow sweetness you've never tasted before. Tonight you don't need sugar! You feel a comfortable warm breeze on your skin. As the sun lowers in the sky, you see harbor lights begin to appear and twinkle like little stars. As it gets darker, you hear a few tentative whistles and snaps. Fireworks! Fireworks are going off from a barge out in the harbor!

The fireworks are shooting, popping, fizzing, twirling and bursting. You hear whistles, hums, hisses, crackles, bangs and booms. There is a kaleidoscopic mix of bright colors shooting, spinning, falling and hanging in the air. You feel the breeze again, and you can begin to smell and even taste the crisp, bittersweet, warm smoke from gunpowder and burnt paper. During the finale, there's a crescendo moment when they fire off the most impressive pieces. You see the sky lit up and feel the deep booming sounds in your chest. You can even hear the sound of your coffee cup rattling in its saucer. In a flash, you think of the first fireworks you ever saw as a child, and for some reason, a thought of your mother appears.

The show fizzles to an end and people applaud. You get up, pay your check, glance out one last time at the harbor and leave.

2 Inquiry into the crescendo. This is a very intense moment. Lots of things seem to be happening at once. Of course, we believe that we can hear something at the exact same time that we see something. But is this actually our experience? Let's make the situation richer, with more kinds of input. If we look at the fireworks display in terms of the kinds of arisings we have spoken about in most of this book (thoughts, feelings, colors, sounds, etc.), then here is an example of what seems to arise all at one instant:

- Sounds
- Colors
- Scents (gunpowder, burnt paper)
- Flavors (coffee, gunpowder, burnt paper)
- Bodily sensations (slight concussive pressure in the chest)
- Thoughts (about childhood and mother and maybe "This is very loud.")

In fact, if you are asked to describe the crescendo, you may feel tempted to say, "It all seemed to happen at once." It seems like it takes a lot longer to remember and describe it all than it took to actually happen.

3 But what is your direct experience in the moment? Let's consider these two possibilities:

(a) At the time, we actually experience the fireworks display to arise as a **multiplicity** of arisings: sounds, colors, scents, sensations and thoughts. And later we recall it as a multiplicity of arisings.

(b) At the time, we actually experience the fireworks display as **one** arising. And later we recall it in terms of a multiplicity of arisings.

Like most of us, my e-mail correspondent would choose (a) and say that for this reason, various mental objects are really real, because they are really different. If mental objects are real, then there is a real seer and real objects being seen. This would perpetuate suffering because of attachment to a separate identity – that of a "seer."

But is (a) really true? How can we choose between (a) and (b)?

Can we use memory to decide between them? No, because we have already found in Experiment 19 that memory is not really memory. It doesn't do what it is advertised to do. It is always unverifiable. There is no verifiable connection between an earlier arising and a later memory-arising that refers to it. So memory can't help us look back "accurately" at the fireworks display. (We will come to discover there's no "earlier" or "later" in experience either.) In fact, this is a feature of all thought. There is no verifiable connection between any thought about an object and an object itself. The "object" is *one* object, and the "thought about the object" is *another* object. These objects touch awareness but never touch each other. Memory and conceptual thought-objects have no place to point other than to awareness itself.

Even if we "remember" the fireworks display as a multiplicity, we have no way of verifying whether it actually was experienced as a multiplicity or as one large lump! Memory will not help us here.

So why do we prefer (a) so strongly? Why did my e-mail correspondent prefer (a) so strongly? There are two usual reasons that we want to insist that colors are one thing, sounds are another thing, flavors and textures are other things, etc.

(i) One reason is that a thought says so. A thought says, "Colors are different from sounds, and one color is different from another," etc. But outside this thought, no difference is directly experienced. This is what we realized in Experiment 20.

(ii) We think that we experience through the body. We think that the body provides us with various corridors or channels of experience through which data can travel simultaneously. If we really experience through the body, and the body really has the sense modalities of vision and hearing, then colors and sounds must be different from each other. And colors and sounds must be as real as the body and its sense modalities. We even suspect that there are other categories of experience that humans don't have. We think that maybe animals, insects and extraterrestrials have other senses, but we can't be totally sure. This adds to our sense of alienation.

But we discovered in Part 2 that we never experience the body as a biological, physical object in the first place. We never directly experience the body to ever perform any function. *We never directly experience ourselves experiencing the world through the body*. The body is experienced. It is not the experiencer. We never experience an *object* (the eye, for example) to be the *subject* (the seer). The seer is awareness, the nature of our very self.

So without the assumption that we experience through the body, the rug has been pulled out from under our assumption that there is an objective difference between types of mental objects.

We have no more reason to experience or regard any mental object as belonging to a "type," and have no experience of any object as separate.

It is a tradition in the Direct Path to say that objects arise one at a time. We have seen that there is no direct evidence that they arise more than one at a time. We will even find out that there is no direct evidence that they arise even one at a time. But that comes later. For now, however, we still need the arisings-model to help us investigate the mind and other subtle objects. This will allow us to discover experientially that we are nothing other than witnessing awareness. And after that point, the entire gestalt and seemingness of "arisings" will dissolve spontaneously into nondual pure consciousness.

Fireworks Display!

But can't various objects arise simultaneously? We will cover this situation at the end of this section on mental objects. For now, just ponder this. How can you tell the difference in direct experience between (a) four thoughts happening simultaneously and (b) a single thought that says, "Thoughts 1, 2, 3, 4 are arising together and they look like this..."?

Conclusion To Mental Objects

We are close to transcending the mind. Of course, we know *theoretically* that "I am not the mind," but is this our direct experience?

What we experience ourselves to be depends on what we feel objectively exists. If we think the world is physical, then we take ourselves as a physical body which perceives the physical world. If we feel that the world is mental (made of thoughts, feelings and desires), then we take ourselves as a separate mind that cognizes the mental world.

If we experience the world as awareness, then we experience ourselves as awareness.

So we are close to transcending the mental – that is, close to no longer taking the mental as objectively real, and close to no longer seeing ourselves as a mental object or function. We have discovered that there are no mental objects that exist objectively. In direct experience, all the so-called thoughts, feelings and desires are nothing more than arisings in awareness. This discovery helps us no longer take ourselves as a separate cognizer of the mental.

Up until this point in our user guide, we have proceeded using a sort of phenomenological vocabulary. We have spoken in terms of colors, sounds, thoughts, feelings and sensations. This vocabulary was used in our inquiry and helped us realize that we never directly experience external objects such as bridges or buildings, or internal objects such as the memory or the subconscious mind. We have also realized that we never experience a gap or a difference between "external" and "internal." So we no longer have a reference point called "the body" that can separate sounds from colors, ears from eyes, and hearing from sound.

Because we have no basis for putting these objects into separate categories, we can speak of all these objects as arisings in awareness. But this doesn't mean that we are taking our present vocabulary literally either. It will serve us at this stage of the investigation, but we will see that it will also be seen through in a very similar way.

Nondual inquiry is very free and flexible. It shifts gears. In traditional Advaita-Vedanta, it is said that the inquirer or the teacher "switches levels" frequently, sometimes even in the same sentence. In our direct inquiry here, our terms helped us get this far, and we are about to leave many of these terms behind. They have done their job. Nondual inquiry leaves no stone unturned, and no entity or phenomenon is ever directly experienced as objective or separate.

Mental Structures

Part of our feeling of separation comes from thinking that the mind has hidden structures that are not directly accessible. This inaccessibility makes us feel divided and separated within ourselves, and separated from others as well, even when we are pretty sure that we are not bodies.

Examples of hidden structures can be seen in the following common beliefs, which may not all be consistent with each other:

- A current thought comes from the subconscious and may be controlled by a hidden motive, which we cannot directly observe.

- The subconscious can't be directly observed, but it is where memories, thoughts and feelings lie hidden.

- Repression and suppression are processes that separate the visible from the invisible in us.

- The subconscious is an ultimately dark featureless structure. During deep sleep, coma, periods of unconsciousness – at these times, the subconscious stores all the contents of the conscious mind.

- The "memory" is where our past resides.

- The "heart" is a structure where emotions reside.

- The "intellect" is a structure where the functions of thinking and judging reside.

I remember learning these concepts in school or when I learned about New Age psychology.

One thing struck me immediately, even as a youngster. That is, these structures sounded like physical objects! They are said to cause things, cover things, enclose things, hold things, suppress things and release things. They are supposed to be separate from each other, which to me usually implied walls between them. These concepts were not presented as metaphors or hypothetical constructs like "gravity" or "force," but as scientific literal truths about the mind.

It was natural for me to visualize these structures – "subsconscious," "unconscious," "memory" and "intellect" – as analogous to physical objects. The best I could come up with was to see them as balloon-like containers with walls consisting of cellular membranes.

Of course, now we can see that as non-physical these "structures" cannot contain anything. Talk of containment and inclusion cannot be literal.

Spiritual Teachings Also Propose Structures

It's not just our school systems that divide the mind. Spiritual teachings do as well. Many years ago, I studied a Rosicrucian system that divides the person into **49 levels**! Most of these are mental levels. I actually liked this teaching very much. It was from Max Heindel, author of **The Rosicrucian Cosmo-Conception**, published in 1909. This esoteric system was able to account for everything I had observed in my life, plus more, such as some additional clairvoyant and mystical experiences that I had not had. Just learning this Rosicrucian system helped me lessen my attachment to the so-called "scientific" account of the mind that I had grown up learning.

Lists of mental structures vary, depending on the teaching. In addition to the conscious, subconscious and memory we have mentioned, there are also structures such as tantric channels and winds, Chinese meridians and points of "chi" convergence, the astral and desire bodies, the third and fourth sheaths or koshas from Hinduism (*manamaya kosha* and *vijnanamaya kosha*), the unconscious, the memory, the "heart-mind," the "I-Am," the soul, the spirit, and the various parts linked to dissociated or split personalities. We can also include the Western anatomic structures (because they are thought to be the physical counterpart of the mind), such as the brain and nervous system (even though they are "physical" structures): cerebrum, cerebellum, limbic system, brain stem, autonomic nervous system, sympathetic nervous system, parasympathetic nervous system, central nervous system and peripheral nervous system.

The Reality Effect

Mental structures can have a fairly strong reality effect. We believe that even though we don't really observe these structures, they nevertheless lie behind what we do observe, conditioning the appearances. If our notions of the mind come from popular psychology, then we probably think the mind is divided into a conscious region and a subconscious region. If we have emotional trouble with something, we attribute it to blockages in the subconscious region even though we never directly observe these blockages. Even though we don't have regular direct access to this region, we still believe in it. This can make us feel separate and divided against ourselves.

But Do We Experience Structures?

Let's take a look at the structure with the strongest reality effect for most people who grew up in the West: the subconscious. The subconscious is thought to be the staging area for most of what goes on in the mind. Most of what is consciously experienced is said to have queued up in the subconscious before seeing the light of day. The subconscious is defined as inaccessible, so we shouldn't expect to peer into it to see its contents. But we can test to see if we observe any thought entering or leaving the subconscious. Let's take a close look.

Experiment 22 – Finding The Subconscious

Purpose – Discovering whether we directly experience the subconscious, which is the paramount example of a structure that is supposed to exist within the mind. If direct experience does not verify the subconscious, then we don't need to take it as the literal truth of our experience.

Objects needed – A chair.

Setup – Sit quietly in the chair.

The Experiment – Begin with the Heart Opener.

1 Think of a thought or experience that we would normally say is buried in the subconscious: Try to remember or imagine a situation when you wanted to remember something, but it wouldn't come. It could be a name, a movie title, a word, or a technique on the computer. "Hmm, who played opposite Humphrey Bogart in **Casablanca?** Who was it? It was on the tip of my tongue!" According to the popular psychological model, that item must be buried in the subconscious. Actually, according to the popular psychological model of experience, *any* thought or experience that you are not currently having is now in the subconscious.

2 Allow the buried item to arise: Remember or imagine the item finally "coming to the surface." AHA! It comes to mind! "Ingrid Bergman!" I think you'll be able to come up with a situation like that. Allow this "buried" object to arise. There was a moment when it wasn't yet present. Then it arose. Try to catch this thought or object arising (or imagine it this way). Try to observe where it is coming from.

3 Allow it to remain, then to subside: Whatever arises will subside after a while. Try to experience the disappearance of this thought or object. Try to observe what it is subsiding back into.

4 Repeat as necessary: You might have to do this several times in order to get clear on just what you experience. What is your direct experience in this process?

Inquiry

- In Step 1, before the object had arisen, did you directly experience the object to be contained or located in the subconscious?

▪ In Step 2, while the object was arising, did you directly experience the object arising *from* the subconscious? I used to imagine this process as like a fish emerging from a pond. But I never observed anything like this happening. But maybe you do. Do you directly experience part of the thought emerge, then more of the thought emerge, until the entire thought is accessible to the conscious mind? Notice that even if you do observe something like this, the observation is nothing other than an arising in awareness.

What you are trying to accomplish is directly experiencing the object to arise from the "subconscious." The subconscious has been proposed by psychology so as to allow us to talk about why some thoughts or feelings seem to arise easily and others seem to have trouble. With the notion of the subconscious, we are able to speak of functions such as suppression and repression of desires, fears and motives. This model and these terms might help with psychological therapies, regardless of whether they are literally true. Our mission here, however, is to search for the literal truth of our experience, to find out whether we actually experience the subconscious directly.

▪ In Step 2, if it seems as though you are witnessing the object arising from the subconscious, then how do you know it is the "subconscious"? For the subconscious to be directly experienced, it must be knowingly and directly experienced *as* the subconscious. If you observe something and then later call it the subconscious, then what you observe is merely a process of naming and not the subconscious itself. You can't be sure that the first object is truly the subconscious, to which the second object (the label) gets applied after the fact. It's not as though you see the subconscious and the label apart from each other, and then together.

▪ In Step 3, did you directly experience the object descending back into the subconscious?

▪ In any of the steps, did you experience a limited structure that held, enclosed, released or accepted your thoughts? Do you directly experience any backstage area, regardless of what it is called? This is very similar to the question, "Do you experience anything unexperienced?"

But isn't this just like witnessing awareness? We don't see it either. It also doesn't carry a label that says, "Hey, I'm witnessing awareness, and arisings come from me!"

What Right Have We To Say That Anything Comes From Witnessing Awareness?

You probably did not experience any object arising from the subconscious or any other mental structure. Mental structures are not your experience. Because they are not your experience, you don't need to believe that the mind is an object with hidden structures inside. To that extent, you don't need to feel separated by structures and divisions you have no access to.

This is true. But there is one big difference. Witnessing awareness is not like the subconscious, which is one structure of several that we believe the mind contains. Nothing contains witnessing awareness. Witnessing awareness cannot be an object, structure or function. It is like the "unseen seer." If we saw it, it would only be another object.

Wherever there is anything seen, witnessing awareness needs to be present, as presence. Witnessing awareness *can't* be seen, just like the knife cannot cut itself.

So it is very simple. What arises is seen. To arise is to be seen. What is seen needs a seer. The seer can't be seen, for then it would be an object, and what would see *this* seer? But there is no infinite regress here, because witnessing awareness is never an object, so it needs no seer. It is the unseen seer. The unseen seer isn't an arising, but that to which arisings appear.

The Sense That I Am The Seer

There is an intuitive connection here as well. We always think that we are the seer, not the seen. I don't mean being the seer in a visual sense, but in the sense that "I am what appearances appear to." Think of any case of an appearance or arising that appears to witnessing awareness. There seems to be the appeared-to and the appearance, the seer and the seen. If we had to choose which of the two we are, we always think of ourselves on the side of the seer. This is the deeply intuitive sense that this unseen seer is "I." It seems like whatever is seen is seen by this "I." It seems that this "I" and the unseen seer are one and the same thing. Since we can't see witnessing awareness, we have no direct experience that witnessing awareness is separated or divided. Our experience is one, whole, global. Even through deep sleep (see 'Note About Deep Sleep' below) we never have the sense that this "I" stops existing or becomes shut off.

This I, this seer, is continuous even though it is not an arising object. In fact, it **has** to be this way. Anything that is seen is discontinuous. Whatever is seen comes and goes. It never remains forever. It's not that we see the seer as continuous. It is the clarity of seeingness itself, which we never see to be interrupted.

Conclusion To Mental Structures

We never experience mental structures. Even if the notion of a mental structure ego arises (such as "the memory" or "the subconscious" or "the superego"), there is nothing experienced aside from this very notion. This notion is nothing more than an arising in witnessing awareness.

Mental Functions

By "mental functions" I mean all the powers and activities the mind is thought to have and the things it is thought to be able to *do*. This would include thinking, feeling, doing, realizing, understanding, believing, desiring, imagining, speaking, seeing, hearing, smelling, touching, tasting, willing, attending, intending, choosing, remembering, forgetting, opening, closing, intuiting, guessing, reasoning, drifting off, focusing, letting go, grasping, attaching, sleeping, waking, appreciating, loving, hating, approaching, avoiding, developing, dissipating, assimilating, accepting, rejecting, balancing, etc.

Mental functions can seem to be subtle and slippery. We seem to "be" some of them, such as the knowing or the doing. We seem to own and control some of these functions, but others seem to control us or go their own way. And sometimes we attribute the present feelings to a mental function that is running "behind the scenes." Any time this happens and we are not pleased with our current state, we feel that the controlling mental function is some sort of enemy. We'd like to control it, but we can't seem to! This causes more alienation and suffering.

Choosing, Doing

Choosing and doing are two of the most common examples of mental functions that masquerade as what we really are. In my own inquiry I searched many years for what I was. After several years, I had narrowed it down to one thing: I felt I was that which chooses. This was in the early 1990s, before I ever encountered Wei Wu Wei's teachings, or those from Ramesh Balsekar, Wayne Liquorman, Tony Parsons or others who specialize in refuting this function. I arrived at this based on my own inquiry and traditional teachings, I think because this sense was very strong in me.

For me, the identification as the chooser was powerful. I landed on this because in looking throughout experience for my sense of self, choosing seemed to be where it lay. I didn't think I was my body or memories or values or thinking or knowledge. It was the chooser where I felt at home. Whenever I felt most to be a specific me was a moment when I had to make a tension-filled decision. All my identity seemed to become involved in the process of choosing. The function of choosing felt as if reflected most of the specific properties that seemed to make me into a separate individual.

And when I felt most free of specificity was when I felt most free from choosing. It was where things seemed to go their own way. These were times where I felt very free and very connected to everything. Joining the U.S. Army in 1975 is an example of this. It's a strange example, because joining the Army is not usually the sort of thing that makes people feel free! But for me it was one long powerful sense of flowing freedom. Events and activities flowed past, diaphanous and zone-like. From the moment the idea was first suggested by a teacher in college, to the excitement, the romanticized memories of WWII and Korean War movies, to the research I did, the conversations with the recruiter, the fantasies he sold me of working in a glamorous foreign embassy, the written entrance tests, raising my right hand to swear in, the airplane flight to boot camp, the experience of getting off the bus to be greeted by the shouting drill sergeant, the first bald-head haircut, the first ill-fitting uniform, the feelings of camaraderie, frustrations and accomplishment – all this felt free and devoid of identity.

So this is an example of how a mental function can seem like the key to one's specific identity, and freedom from this mental function is experienced as freedom from identity.

So let's look to see whether the function of choosing actually does exist. Is there truly a function that exists, a function that actually **does** something?

Experiment 23 – Finding The Choosing Function

We will investigate the choosing function by examining the choice between two different beverages. It's best to be a little bit thirsty for this one!

Purpose – To discover whether the choosing function can really be found or verified in direct experience. "Choosing" is a very clear example of a function that we mis-identify as the basis of our identity. But if choosing cannot be found, then this function cannot be what we really are, and we are freed from it.

Objects needed – A chair, a table and two different beverages. They can be any two beverages that you would like to drink right now, including coffee, tea, milk, water, fruit juices, vegetable juices, smoothies, protein shakes, beer, wine, etc. For the sake of convenience, I will use "coffee" and "tea" while describing this experiment.

Setup – Place the two beverages side by side on the table in front of you. Sit quietly in the chair. We will examine the choice between two different beverages.

The Experiment – Begin with the Heart Opener.

1 Look at each one, the coffee and the tea: feel your desire for one of the choices, then the other. Think about the qualities you like. Make any comparisons you wish. Weigh and balance the qualities of the two drinks.

2 Count to 5.

3 Choose one of the drinks. Pick it up and take a sip. Aaahh!

Inquiry

▪ We are looking for a choosing function. In Step 1, where you felt the desire-arisings for coffee, then for tea (or whatever you actually used in the experiment), did you in that moment *choose* the desire-arisings? Did you directly experience a desiring or choosing function? If so, what did it look like? If it was a feeling, then did you directly experience that feeling to make a choice? Is choosing something that feelings actually do? Did you witness a feeling performing such a function? What does that look like? Do feelings actually consider and choose things? Or is it just a thought that says so?

▪ In Step 2, where you counted to 5, if the desires you felt in Step 1 diminished and numbers appeared, did you *choose* this turn of events? Did you choose that the desires would subside and the numbers appear? Did you directly experience a choosing function appear and operate on the desires and the numbers? Did you see it in action?

▪ In Step 3, where you made a choice, did you actually witness or directly experience a mental function or faculty doing the choosing? Did anything arise that announced, "I am the chooser"? If so, what does that choosing function look like? Again, for it to really be a function, it has to be something other than a feeling. If you did directly experience a function, what was it like? Did it have color or shape or a characteristic sound or vibratory pattern? Can that same function arise in other circumstances, say, when you are choosing to get up out of bed and go to work in the morning?

To Do On Your Own

The attachment to being the chooser is quite a strong one. You may wish to do other experiments with different kinds of choice situations. Can you directly experience the existence of a choosing function? These experiments are also helpful even if you are not really in the situation currently, but are recalling the situation from having gone through it in the past:

- When you want something like a new computer or pair of shoes or car, "Hmmm, do I buy this inexpensive one now or save for a better one later?"

- On a weekend, "Do I stay in bed or get up?"

- After high school or college, "OK, what is next in life – more school or a job?"

- Choosing a place to live.

- Choosing between two prospective lovers.

- Choosing a spiritual path.

- Choosing to meditate or not.

Why You Can't Directly Experience The Choosing Function

In general, if anything arises as the chooser, it is never by direct experience, but by hearsay. Something is announcing something else as the chooser. Some arising X happens. Then some arising Y happens that says, "X is the chooser." When Y is pointing, X is nowhere to be found and cannot be pointed to. It might seem to you that an arising announces itself as the chooser. "I am the chooser." Let's call it arising Z. But no arising can self-announce as choosing. Why not? Because that arising is just "announcing," it is not "choosing." There is a claim that seems to happen, but the referent of the claim is not present.

So not only **do you not** directly experience choosing as a function, **you cannot** directly experience it. The closest you can get to directly experiencing the choosing function is when an arising appears that seems to make this claim. But as we have seen many times in our inquiry, none of these claims is ever verified. At most, there is a thought that says so.

Freedom From Choice

In realizing that there is no choosing that is directly experienced to happen, there can be fear. It can feel like a loss of control. But you never lost control because you never had it to begin with. Persons don't have control – persons, like "control" and "loss of control," are nothing other than spontaneous arisings in you, as awareness. All of this comes and goes freely in you. "Choice" is always free, and so are you. This is no different from realizing that the world and body are simply awareness. You are free from all these things because all they are is awareness, which is you.

Having realized this, you don't need to talk funny and tell co-workers, plumbers and accountants that there is no world or body or choice. Life flows spontaneously and freely. The everyday language may continue to arise. You will not be bound by it, but will celebrate its freedom, and yours.

The Attention

Closely related to the notion of choosing is the notion of attention. In the everyday sense of speaking, it seems like attention is a focus that we can direct as we wish. We understand ourselves to be able to look at or listen to what we want, and to think about what we wish to think about. Because we think the mind controls the senses the way a hand controls a flashlight, we think we are able to focus the scrutiny of "looking" and "listening" in any direction we want.

At a movie, we can focus on any one actor, or broaden the focus to incorporate the entire scene. We can look at the scenery, the colors, the extras, or even focus on the screen as the bearer of the projected image. We can direct our attention to the music, the ambient sounds in the film or the seats in the theater. We can focus on the ideas being discussed in the dialogue, the accents or the linguistic choices of the screenwriter. We can attend to the plot, action, pace, color palette, camera work or location. It seems very easy to switch our attention from one thing to another.

Not only can we change the direction of our attention, but also the breadth and intensity. We can look at the center of the screen or broaden the focus to encompass the entire screen. We can listen to one sound tone or instrument from the score or the entire range of sound. Our attention can be hard and laser-intense, or soft and open.

Sometimes the attention seems not to be directed by our choice, but seems pulled in various directions by the events themselves.

Attention seems like an extremely articulate beam of sentient energy that can be modulated in infinite ways, either through our choosing or by other means. In spiritual teaching we are sometimes taught to use the attention in different ways or even to focus on the attention itself. Learning to meditate is partly learning to work with the attention.

But what is our direct experience of attention? Attention is very much like choice. It seems to be something that we can do. But in direct experience it is an object that arises. Let's take the example of changing our attention at a movie:

1 You look at the actors, because there is someone there who looks very interesting.

2 Some action begins, so you really focus on the action. You begin to critique the car chase, because it looks fake. "Real cars don't do that!"

3 You realize that the characters seem to be saying something important, so you switch your attention to the dialogue. You think that this bit of dialogue may be important for the plot.

4 You hear noises behind you and switch your attention away from the movie to the theater behind you. You realize that people are talking a few rows back. You hear someone else hissing "SSShhhh," and the talking stops. You switch your attention back to the movie.

At each stage your attention moves from one thing to another. Sometimes this happens as though by your will, and sometimes by other means.

But what is your direct experience? In each case, the attention is an object arising to witnessing awareness.

- Attending to something is nothing more than the arising of a feeling of concentration, a feeling of closure or containment, and perhaps the conceptual sense that "I am focusing on this." These feelings and senses are nothing more than arisings appearing to witnessing awareness.

- Explicitly switching your attention from one thing to another is nothing more than the arising of several feelings. There may be a feeling of intent, a feeling of changing your perception from one object to another. There may be a sense of control here, the sense that you accomplished this change through your own intent. This "switching" is analogous to the case of doership that we examined in Experiment 23 above. All these feelings and senses are spontaneous, unchosen arisings in awareness.

- When the attention seems to switch on its own, without your control, it is still a set of spontaneous arisings in awareness. This time, however, there is just no arising that seems to say, "I am doing this."

Conclusion To Mental Functions

We do not need to investigate other mental functions. Of course, you can investigate as many of them on your own as you like. We chose the choosing function because it is so commonly thought to be the basis of our identity. But different people may feel a stronger pull from different functions. Most people feel that if they can find *any* function, it would be choosing. But if we can't find choosing, then how could we find other more slippery functions like thinking, willing or desiring? Choosing seems obvious and easy to pinpoint, at least before we did this experiment. If choosing were really there, we should be able to experience it directly. But we can't.

The other mental functions are like this. They are nothing more than certain arisings in awareness along with arisings that purport to label them. But none of this can be found when we look deeply for it in direct experience. You can set up other experiments if you would like, and try to find other functions. If you do, it will most likely confirm and solidify your realization.

We are coming closer to freedom from mind. We have just discovered that the mind cannot consist of mental functions. We will next investigate mental states.

Mental States

By "mental states" I mean the conditions or modes of being that are thought to pertain to the underlying mind.

Mental states are the life of the party. They have a very powerful reality effect. For many people, having better mental states is the whole purpose of the spiritual search. We want to avoid the state of suffering and attain the state of happiness. Nothing can seem more real than these! And the sense of difference between **what we have** and **what we want** is also very real and a powerful cause of suffering.

But if you learn through direct experience that you never actually find a mental state in the first place, then you will be free from seeking mental states. This is a huge liberation, and this liberation is necessary in order to no longer identify yourself as the mind.

OK, then just what mental states are there?

Lists of states come from various philosophies, psychologies and spiritual traditions. States can include emotional states like fear, pride, shame, anger, indignation, resentment, desire, hope, bliss, happiness, contentment and peace. They can include the intellectual states of belief, disbelief, confusion, doubt, certainty, inquiry, wonderment, suspicion and querying. States can also include how we summarize what is going on with the mind overall, such as waking, dreaming, deep sleep, trance, coma, semi-consciousness, unconsciousness, haziness, cloudiness, sharpness. And they can include a variety of moral or ethical states such as good, evil, cruelty, kindness, gratitude, envy, indignation, tolerance, trust, deception and self-deception, forgiveness, hypocrisy, honesty and dishonesty, etc.

Mental states can include various spiritual states such as wisdom, ignorance, enlightenment, salvation, grace, faith, one-pointedness, kindness, mindfulness, attentiveness, suppleness, concentration, conscientiousness and *bodhicitta*. There are also meditative states from various traditions. From Buddhism, there are the increasingly subtle *rupa jhanas* (the four meditative states with form) and *arupa jhanas* (the four meditative states without form). From Hinduism, there are meditative states such as *savikalpa samadhi, nirvikalpa samadhi, sahaja samadhi*, as well as Patanjali's six samadhis with a meditative object (the *savitarka, nirvitarka, savichara, nirvichara, sananda* and *sasmita* samadhis), and the one kind of samadhi without a meditative object (*nirbija* **samadhi**).

If we included more traditions and theories, this list would only grow!

That Sounds TIRING! What Is Our Direct Experience?

I actually elaborated those examples just so that it would sound exhausting. So many states and schemes! And it only gets worse if we include more traditions. Is our direct experience this complicated? No!

Mental states don't even exist. A mental state is very much like the (other) mental objects that we already examined. The difference would be that a state is supposed to last longer. We already saw that mental objects are never directly experienced – that when you look closely at what is given in direct experience, you never find anything more than an arising in awareness. And we will end up finding less as we go forth.

But are states any different? Are they perhaps a quality of the mind, like an adjective or a color value? Let's see if we can actually find a mental state in direct experience!

Experiment 24 – Looking For The State Of An Active Mind

We will investigate the mental state of the mind being active. It seems that there are times when the mind is active and other times when it is sluggish. Just think about the difference that a cup of coffee is supposed to make! But when we really look for this state, is it really given in direct experience?

Purpose – To discover whether the "active" mental state can really be found. If not, then there is one less reason to believe that states, and the mind, are objectively real. We will lose the incentive to mis-identify ourselves as these things.

Objects needed – A chair. A pen. A piece of paper.

Setup – Sit quietly in the chair. We will look for the state of being mentally active.

The Experiment – Begin with the Heart Opener.

1 If the mind is active right now, then you can use the current "state" in your inquiry. If your mind doesn't feel very active right now, then just try to remember a time when the mind was active. It can be a time when you were very busy or frantic, or had a lot of thoughts or inner dialog.

2 Just what makes this state seem active? How are you distinguishing this state from a state of being inactive? Write down all the characteristics that make this state seem active. They could include:

- Thoughts come more quickly.
- I feel more energy.
- Sensations appear lighter and more vibrant.
- I can remember names, words and ideas that I usually cannot remember.
- My usual pessimistic outlook seems to have lifted.

3 Now try to separate three things from each other.

- *Characteristics:* These are the things you noticed that made you feel like your mind was active. They might include characteristics such as having lots of rapid-fire thoughts in a short period of time, or a feeling of being pulled in many directions at once, or a feeling that you are thinking faster than you usually do.

- *State:* Try to find the state that the characteristics point to. This would probably be the state of activity, of being frantic, of feeling that your attention span is very short. If it is a state, it is thought to somehow describe how you are doing right now.

- *Mind:* Try to find the mind that is in this state.

Inquiry

- In Step 1, notice that you were thinking about mental states in a very ordinary way. There seemed to be no problem, and there was no deep investment or belief necessary in order to think about the state of an active mind. (The fact that we don't need to think about our mind can be a helpful teaching in any case!) We didn't really start looking closely into this state until Step 2. The everyday approach in Step 1 is indeed the same sort of conventional, everyday approach that can occur with everything we have looked into, beginning with physical objects.

- In Step 2, you wrote down many characteristics of the active state of mind. Notice that all these characteristics are thoughts, feelings, sensations, "states" or other arisings, or they are references to them. No matter how long one's list, it is a list that refers to arisings only. The list itself is an arising. So in all these arisings, just where does one find the direct experience of the state of an "active mind"? Here we are not approaching the state in a conventional everyday manner, but in a spirit of inquiry, in which we check for the truth of our experience. Have we found a state of mind? No.

- In Step 3, we are trying to make the notion of "a state of mind" become more clear. If the state of mind is analogous to the state of a thermometer, or to the state of a computer being on or off, then we should be able to directly experience the various components: mind, state and characteristics of the state.

Experiment 25 – Looking For A Bad Mood

Purpose – To discover whether the mental state of a "bad mood" can really be found. A bad mood is something that seems like a very palpable and obvious state of mind. You feel impatient, easily irritated. You are quick to anger. You yearn to feel better. You keep thinking of the argument you had at home in the morning, and then the dismissive and threatening treatment you received from your boss at work. It seems that if any mental state can be found, it would be a bad mood!

But if we can't find the state of being in a bad mood, then we won't have to struggle to extricate ourselves from a bad mood the next time it seems to arise. We will be closer to not attaching to a good mood, which will help with no longer identifying with the mind.

Objects needed – A chair.

Setup – Sit quietly in the chair. We will look for the state of being in a bad mood. It can be a present or past instance. You may wish to remember a bad mood that you were in previously.

The Experiment – This time, **do not** begin with the Heart Opener, since we're trying to tune into a bad mood! You can do the Heart Opener after the experiment.

1 If you are in a bad mood by any chance, then use this mood in your inquiry. If you are not in a bad mood, try to recall a previous instance of a bad mood. It can be from any time in your life. The most important thing is that you can recall it vividly. See what you saw at the time. Feel what you felt. Was there a sour taste in your mouth? Was your stomach upset? What were you thinking about? Did you feel like you wanted to curl up into a ball and go to sleep?

2 What are the feelings that arise? Are there stories that arise? Are there preferences arising also, according to which you wish to be saved from this mood and magically changed to be in a better mood? Take note of these feelings, stories and preferences, allowing them to be as vivid as they wish to be.

3 After taking note of what arises during the mood, allow these feelings, stories and preferences, if any, to subside. If the feelings persist, you can even do the Heart Opener at this point.

Inquiry

▪ Notice that in Step 1, you began by not being in a bad mood. You experienced a time in which the particular feelings associated with this bad mood had not arisen just yet. In Step 2, the feelings arose and abided for a time. In Step 3, the feelings diminished or subsided. Did you directly experience those feelings, stories and preferences before (and after) they were "on stage"? Did you experience them to be somewhere other than in awareness? If so, where could that be?

- Notice that in Step 2, you may casually say that the feelings making up the mood were present. But were they really? In many of our earlier experiments, you have had the experience of looking for feelings and thoughts and not being able to find them.

- So can you find the feelings in this case? Let's say you "find" an anxious, jittery, angry feeling. Let's look closer. What are the components of this feeling? Of course, we know that there is a label, called "feeling" or "anger." But besides the label (which is an object in awareness), just what do you find that constitutes the anger? Fast heartbeat? Fast breathing? Images of you taking revenge on your boss? All of these can be nothing more substantial than objects arising in awareness. As we have seen, the body is not something that breathes or jitters. The bodily structures and movements are nothing more than arisings in awareness, and as such, they are nothing other than awareness itself.

- But are they really even objects? Are they the sort of thing that you directly experience as being present or absent? As we have seen over and over – when you truly look closely for an object, you cannot find it. When it seems to be "there," you can't actually find it because there is nothing to grab hold of. It is not present to look at – it is at zero distance from you as witnessing awareness. It's as though you are in the eye of a hurricane. The object simply cannot be verified in direct experience. And when the object seems not to be there, then its presence cannot be verified. The label that calls out "anger" is not the anger, but merely a label functioning as an accusation. But where is the supposed referent of the label?

- It seems that the only time that it makes sense to say that you are "in a bad mood" is when you can look as if from some distance apart from that state and make a statement about it. But the statement is not the state. The state is not directly experienced and cannot be found apart from the statement. And if we went looking for the statement, it is not directly experienced either.

Conclusion To Looking For A Bad Mood

▪ The purpose of this experiment is to try to directly experience the mind by directly experiencing characteristics of the mind, such as mental states. In order for the mind to actually be in a state, we need to be able to find and distinguish three things:

▪ *Characteristics:* The thoughts and feelings and sensations that seem to define the state. These experiences are usually thought to be "symptoms" of the state (if it is very unpleasant). If your state is a bad mood, then what experiences are happening that seem to define or make up this state? Can you locate them through direct experience?

▪ *State:* The state itself, apart from the characteristics, and apart from the mind. What do the characteristics point to? Is there something to the bad mood apart from its characteristics? (For example, think of a car. Is there a "car-ness" that still exists like a form or a template even when all the parts have been removed? This inquiry can be done with any object, physical or mental.) With the bad mood, just what do the characteristics represent? What does the label "bad mood" point to?

▪ *Mind:* That which is supposedly *in* the state. If the mind really exists, you should be able to directly experience it, both in the given state and outside of the state. Do you directly experience the mind in this way?

If you do not directly experience these components of a mind being in mental states, then this is one less reason to take the mind seriously as an existing, independent thing. And this is one less reason to believe and feel that we are the mind. When we look closely, we just can't find the mind in direct experience!

Conclusion To Mental States

There are other mental states that you can investigate on your own. The idea, of course, is always to try to find our self, which we feel has independent, objective existence. If we take ourselves as the mind, then we should be able to find it in direct experience if it really exists the way we think it does. The more kinds of mental states you investigate, the more you will fail to find them, and the more evidence you will find that you are awareness only!

To Do On Your Own

Try replicating this experiment on the following "states," and any others that you can think of:

- The state of being in a good mood
- The state of suffering
- The waking state
- The state of being very tired
- The dream state (i.e., during sleep; you will probably have to use memory here, unless you can do the experiment while "lucid dreaming")
- The state of being *unenlightened* (if you feel that is your current state)
- The state of being *enlightened* (if you feel that is your current state)

Note About Deep Sleep

Not many spiritual teachings pay much attention to deep sleep. The teachings of Vedanta are the only teachings I know of that have a teaching that involves deep sleep.

In traditional Advaita-Vedanta, deep sleep (*sushupti*) is taught to be a state of consciousness very similar to that of the true Self, but it is still a thin, dark covering over the true Self. There is no subject, object or suffering experienced. Deep sleep is blissful because there is no mind, body or world experienced as present. But deep sleep is not the equivalent of self-knowledge. Even though there are no objects experienced in deep sleep, there is also no direct understanding present in deep sleep. It is still a state and a superimposition over one's true nature. One proof that deep sleep is a state is that it comes to an end, whereas our true nature as Awareness never comes to an end. Merely experiencing deep sleep without understanding one's true nature is not enough to realize the Self.

Deep Sleep In The Direct Path

In the Direct Path unlike in traditional Advaita-Vedanta, deep sleep is not a state. Rather, it is one's true nature. It is basically objectless consciousness. It is awareness with no suffering, no arisings, no witnessing, and no mind, body or world. When one wakes up after a good night's sleep, one will say, "Ah... I slept happily!" When you wake up from deep sleep, you did not pass from one state to another. Instead, there was a period of objectless consciousness, which was then followed by the onset of objects. This objectless experience is also available in a cultivated meditative state like **nirvikalpa samadhi.** But deep sleep tends to be available more widely! Both cases are examples of pure "I" or pure presence: awareness with no division between subject and object. When deep sleep comes to an end, this is a case of objects arising. We call that "the waking state."

You don't **witness** deep sleep. You **are** deep sleep. You are the awareness to which arisings may appear, and the awareness is present during arisings, between arisings and beyond arisings.

The goal of one's inquiry is not to always be in deep sleep, but to intuitively understand that one is the very same even now: awareness. One learns from the teaching of deep sleep that one is gently and purely present even though there is no world, body or mind appearing.

This can seem counterintuitive and gives rise to two common questions:

Q: *There seems to be nothing **at all** going on in deep sleep. There is absolutely nothing to remember. How can a teaching say that there was happiness or that I was present?*

A: It's true that there are no experiences of thoughts, feelings or sensations during deep sleep. If there were even the most subtle flickering lights experienced, then by definition this would be a "dream" of some sort and not deep sleep. The reason we say that happiness is present is not that you were feeling bliss or excitement, but rather that there was no suffering or anxiety.

The reason we say that you (as awareness) were present during deep sleep is that there is no sense of absence or of ceasing to exist. You didn't experience yourself to fall out of existence or come back into existence.

You have no sense at all, even after waking up, that you weren't present during deep sleep, even though no objects were present. This is the great lesson of deep sleep – that **you** are, even though **objects** are not.

We say that awareness is "present" in deep sleep, as indeed it always is. But it is not present the way we would think of a currently appearing object being present. An object may appear to be present, but it will soon be absent. Awareness is "present" in a different way. This "present" is a freedom from absence or loss. In deep sleep there is no experience of absence, loss, discontinuity or interruption. It is this presence, this witnessing awareness, that is your nature. Awareness is exactly that presence to which the waking and dream "objects" appear. Awareness is the same presence as deep sleep, to which the objects of waking and dreaming appear when they do. In other words, if awareness were not present, then what would recognize the waking state when it arises?

Q: *But my body is present in deep sleep. I just wasn't aware of it. To prove it, we can set up a video camera and record me while I am sleeping. When we play back the recording, it will prove that my body and the world were there.*

A: In the everyday sense of talking about experience and the world, this makes good sense. Your body can be filmed. Therefore, that is evidence of your presence.

But is it *really*? When we inquire deeply into our direct experience of the world as we did in Part 1, we discover that the world is not experienced as such at all. The world is nothing other than awareness. We see this by discovering that the world is not independent from color, form, sound and texture. These sensations are not independent from seeing, hearing, touching, etc. And seeing, hearing and touching are not independent of witnessing awareness. Awareness is the common denominator of all, the nature of all.

Because the world is nothing more than a set of arisings in witnessing awareness, the world cannot be proven through arisings. One arising cannot prove another arising, since they do not contact, touch or refer to each other, even in memory. So the set of arisings that we call "the video camera" cannot prove the existence of another set of arisings that we call "my body," no matter what colors and shapes appear on the camera's monitor. And even then, arisings that happen during the present are incapable of proving what went on in a past time when deep sleep was occurring. This is because memory in general (as an arising like others) is unable to prove the past as it claims to do. It is merely another arising, and arisings do not contact or communicate with each other.

Arisings in witnessing awareness are never accessed apart from witnessing awareness. The arisings depend on witnessing awareness, but witnessing awareness does not depend on arisings. The proof is deep sleep, where awareness is present in the absence of arisings.

The Goal Of The Teachings On Deep Sleep

The goal of the teaching is not to try to be in deep sleep or trance or *samadhi* forever. Deep sleep is just that interval in which it happens that there are no objects appearing.

The teaching from deep sleep is the discovery that for you to be you do not need objects. You are the same, whether arisings appear or not. Your identity never depends on any arisings whatsoever. If this lesson is deeply understood, then several remarkable things happen:

- You will no longer prefer that some objects arise rather than others, because it will be realized that preferences between objects are still objects.

- You will no longer require that certain objects remain absent. This is because it will be realized that our expectations about what happens to objects are still objects.

- You won't be shaken by the appearance of certain arisings and therefore judge that you "fell out of" nonduality. This is because you realize that a supposed state of being in duality and a supposed state of being in nonduality are themselves objects.

- You will not think that the goal of nonduality is to be in deep sleep forever, because you will realize that you as awareness do not need objects in order to exist, whether they seem to arise or not. Either way, you are awareness. You will not make an object out of the literal absence of objects. The freedom you give to objects to arise or not is a sort of openness and unconditional love towards objects. This leads to the thinning out of objects and to their eventual dissolution.

▪ Deep sleep and trance and moments of insight and being in the "zone" will no longer seem more nondual than other times.

▪ The very notion that objects arise in the first place will begin to make less and less sense.

Experiment 26 – The Happiness Of Deep Sleep

Purpose – To recall the objectless happiness of deep sleep so that you recognize that you are present and free from suffering even though objects aren't present.

Objects needed – A chair.

Setup – Sit quietly in the chair.

The Experiment – Begin with the Heart Opener.

NOTE: If you happen to fall asleep during the experiment on deep sleep, as long as you are in safe surroundings it is perfectly OK! It might even help!

1 Recall a time when you felt dead tired and dropped off into a totally dreamless sleep.

2 Recall the sense of eagerness as you approached the bed. Why were you so eager? Because you had a sense of the relief from exhaustion and the freedom from care that awaited you in deep sleep.

3 Recall if you can waking up after that (or any) episode of deep sleep. There might be the feeling of peace, happiness or a sense of being refreshed. There might be a wish to "go back" into deep sleep again.

4 Contemplate how from the standpoint of waking up right after deep sleep, or from the standpoint of now, you had the sense that you had been present all throughout the time you were sleeping. You never thought you stopped existing and then came back into existence. You never felt your being as interrupted by the period of deep sleep. Even though during deep sleep there were no arisings and hence no evidence of a mind, body or world, you never had the sense that you were not present. When you think about how you exist from day to day, you have a sense that you were there all the time.

5 Contemplate how in the period of deep sleep you must have been present as awareness in order that you "see" arisings once they begin again. You must have already been there as presence which was able to "intercept" the arisings that begin and which constitute the waking state.

Inquiry

▪ Recall from what you have discovered in your inquiry so far that you have no grounds for claiming that "there is a world out there." That is, you have already experienced directly that the world is nothing more than arisings in witnessing awareness. The same goes for the body and mind. The body and mind are also nothing more than arisings in awareness. You have also discovered in the Tent experiment in Part 2 that there can also be no "out there" and no border between "in" and "out."

▪ Realize how, because the world, body and mind are nothing more than arisings, they are not the kind of thing that can persist through deep sleep. There is no way that the world, body and mind can be present during an interval when no arisings are arising.

▪ Realize what this means for you to be present. You are present even though no arisings are present. You cannot possibly be aware of your own absence, because to be at all is to be awareness, which is present as presence. There is no true absence in awareness. There may be a thought that seems to carry a message of absence. But absence itself is never present. What would absence really be?

- Think about several logical possibilities during deep sleep. You are the same awareness *before* and *after* deep sleep. So there are two possibilities compatible with our investigations so far for what happens *during* deep sleep. Either (1) you are present (though not as an object) the whole time. Or (2) you stopped existing during deep sleep but started up again when arisings returned. OK, so how could (2) work? You as awareness stop. But then you, as that very same awareness, return? If you can stop and start like that, then what maintains your identity in between? How do you know for sure that what starts is not something different from what stopped earlier, along with a trick of "memory" that makes it seem the same? So in this case, just what is it that guarantees that you are the same as before and not something different? Another problem with option (2) is that if awareness can stop and start, then there are two of them, not one. And, of course, the biggest problem with option (2) is that it is not your direct experience.

- So if option (2) makes no sense, then you are back to option (1). That is, you are present as awareness throughout all intervals, whether objects arise or not.

The Mind – Conclusion

The mind is more subtle than the body or the world, so it is often easier to get stuck there. That is, it's sometimes difficult to tell the difference between the mind and witnessing awareness. It is possible to take yourself to be witnessing awareness but interpret witnessing awareness in such a way that it is a mind-state or mental function. For this reason, we examined these aspects of the mind and found them to be various sorts of subtle objects arising to witnessing awareness. If something can arise and pass away, then it is not witnessing awareness but an object instead. We are now better equipped to distinguish what arises from THAT to which it arises.

Where We Are Now

If you have followed the inquiry up to this point, you will have discovered through direct experience that you stand as awareness. This stand is nothing that you do. It is "taken" by awareness automatically by virtue of its nature. Through direct experience you have confirmed this stand in many ways. You have discovered that the world, body and mind are not separate from you in any way. You have discovered that every experience "of" the world, body and mind is nothing more than an arising in witnessing awareness.

And there is never any direct experience of any of these things existing outside of awareness, despite what the paradigm of realism argues. You have experienced no inside or outside or border to awareness. Geographical and spatial metaphors no longer make sense as descriptors of your experience.

You have also discovered the global nature of awareness. You know it not to be an object, and not to be divided or segregated from anything. Nothing contains awareness. It is not walled in, so there can't be two or more awarenesses. It isn't even a countable thing. The nonduality of awareness is the nature of your experience at every moment. It is sweet and devoid of separation and suffering.

You have discovered yourself to be this awareness. All other candidates for your identity, such as forms, shapes or functions in the body and mind, have been realized as nothing more than arisings in awareness, which are experienced *as* awareness.

PART 4 – WITNESSING AWARENESS

At this point in the inquiry, you have been established in witnessing awareness, a.k.a. the witness. Witnessing awareness is that to which arisings appear.

You are free from identification with the body or mind. You are free from thinking that there are two or more awarenesses. You no longer suspect that awareness is caused by something in the world, such as the body or brain. There is nothing "in" awareness that ever pulls you "out of" awareness. You don't think that anything needs to refer to or exist outside of awareness even for a fraction of a second. Your experience contains nothing that is not your very Self.

There's an ironic beauty to this as well. By looking for truth, you may have actually found sweetness! Many people search for sensory or emotional sweetness and expect that search to yield the **sweetness of truth**. But that method looks only at the surface of phenomena. In our own investigation we have looked deeper – into truth. Truth is the source of sweetness, and sweetness is the fragrance of truth. This fragrance is a sweet, causeless, formless freedom that doesn't depend on a good mood, money or luck. This freedom isn't shaken by the ups and downs of life. Why not? Because this freedom doesn't come from arisings. It is "inside" them already. This freedom comes from the source of arisings – awareness itself. There is no arising that can hide this freedom or knock it aside.

This is what we call being established in the witness.

But the "witness" shouldn't be taken literally. It doesn't literally exist. It's not an object, a state or a level of consciousness. If you look for it, it won't be found any more than a teacup is found. Instead, the witness is a convenient manner of speaking. It's a way to efficiently summarize how experience seems to be.

The witness is a structural necessity whenever it seems as if there are arisings of any type. If there is an arising, it must be seen. Indeed, this is our experience at every moment. Wherever there is an arising, there is also the seeing of this arising. We never have an arising that is not seen. An unseen arising doesn't even make sense. What sees all arisings is not the person, but this same unbroken, unbordered witnessing awareness. It is your very Self.

Two Kinds Of Witness

Witnessing awareness is usually defined as "the background of all that arises," or "that which is appeared to." These are like the traditional Advaita-Vedantic characterization of the witness as the "unseen seer." It is significant that none of these definitions include any other characteristics. You don't see definitions like "awareness is the cause and creator of arisings" or "awareness is the storehouse of arisings."

Witnessing awareness doesn't do anything or perform any functions. But we often feel as if it does.

To account for this, the Direct Path makes a distinction between two different types of witness. One is the "thick" or "lower" or what I will call "opaque witness." The other is the "thin" or "higher" or what I will call "transparent witness."

As we mentioned above, the witness is not an actual thing or state, so these designations shouldn't be taken literally. They are merely convenient ways to summarize your understanding of experience.

The Opaque Witness

Among people on a path of inquiry, there are often many questions about the witness. What does it do? What does it want? How long does it last? And then what happens? And why? It can seem that witnessing awareness can do things like remembering or managing arisings. If so, then this understanding of witnessing awareness is a "thick" one. It is thickened with characteristics in addition to "being appeared to." Sometimes it is called the "lower" witness. It is especially helpful at the earlier stages of inquiry when you are investigating the difference between the world and the self. At that time, you are looking into physicality, perception and the body. You aren't thinking so much about what witnessing awareness is supposed to be. As you continue your investigation, it is natural that your understanding clarifies, and your understanding of the witness "thins out." You come to attribute less and less to awareness. You personalize it less.

For the purposes of this inquiry, I will call this sort of witness the "opaque" witness. It is opaque because it seems to have some characteristics or functions that you can't observe. But you feel they are somehow there, in the witness.

Another way to approach the notion of the opaque witness is by checking your contentment – if you really don't feel as if you are the body or the mind, but would like a different or better stream of arisings, then you are expecting witnessing awareness to be able to change this. Whatever ability or function it takes to make this change is the characteristic you perhaps think is somehow inside witnessing awareness. I'm calling this witness opaque because of the suspicion that can arise that this functionality is somehow "in" the witness but can't easily be seen or discerned.

And just what are these characteristics that we feel that witnessing awareness has inside it? These characteristics get attributed to the witness because of the different expectations, dissatisfactions and puzzlements we have around awareness. Here is a list of some of the most common ones. You may wonder:

- Can arisings become more pleasant, like those of my spiritual mentors?

- If awareness is love, then why does it allow unlovable arisings to arise?

- Can arisings stop altogether? That would be more nondual. Will awareness lead me there?

- Why are there arisings at all? Why is there something rather than nothing?

- Where do arisings come from? What causes them? Do they cause each other, or does awareness cause them all?

- Why do arisings create the specific patterns they seem to create? Why do things look just *this* way, rather than some other way? What causes this?

- Are arisings governed by space and time?

- Are arisings governed by the laws of logic or mathematics?

- Does witnessing awareness record and remember everything that arises?

- Can an arising arise more than once, or is each one unique? Can two arisings be the same? How does awareness keep all that straight?

- Will awareness help me get to the point when only peaceful arisings arise?

These questions conceptualize witnessing awareness as having abilities and responsibilities. These abilities include managing, controlling, causing, creating, choosing, nurturing, obeying, remembering and making determinations of sameness and difference. Granted, no one can see into awareness to be sure that it has these abilities. This inability to see into awareness, plus our yearning or suspicion that awareness can do these things, is what makes the witness seem opaque.

I have talked to many people over the years who have thought of awareness in these ways. If you look at the items on the list, they begin to look like the same sorts of things we attribute to a mind. Attributing these sorts of abilities to the witness serves to personify it. The opaque witness is a personified witness.

Again, the opaque witness is perfectly natural. It's even helpful at certain stages of your inquiry. You can stand as this comfortable and non-physical "I" while you investigate the world and the body. Based on what you earlier experienced through perception, you are able to see that the embodied "self" is nothing more than a remembered arising, and not a true self. Later, when you investigate witnessing awareness, you will discover that this feature of memory is not actually a function of awareness at all, but just another arising. Because of this discovery, assisted by the opaque witness, the witness becomes more transparent.

Not only is the opaque witness helpful, but there are many nondual teachings that conceptualize it in just this way, as if the characteristics that get attributed to the witness correspond to the final nondual truth. For example, here are some sound-bites from nondual teachings that tend to personify awareness. They may all sound familiar.

- *"Consciousness knew itself but wanted to experience itself. So it emanated phenomenality."*

- *"Consciousness was bored, so it made the world."*

- *"Consciousness wants us to wake up and realize our true nature."*

- *"Consciousness has a plan for your life."*

- *"Consciousness will find you a mate."*

- *"Nothing is lost. Everything you do is recorded in the storehouse of consciousness."*

These pronouncements attribute quite human characteristics to awareness, such as desire, boredom and the abilities to remember, plan and nurture.

Investigating The Opaque Witness

Seeing awareness in this personified way, we expect awareness to make things better for us. But this is dualistically treating awareness as if it were another entity, while treating our self as an entity too. We want this self to be improved by awareness. This is treating our self and awareness as separate.

But is this separation our direct experience? A clue is that nondual teachings state that Awareness is our very self. There can't be two I's, with one seeing the other.

So let's look closely at the opaque witness to see if we directly experience it to have these features and functions as part of its nature.

Desire, Will And Choice

Experiment 27 – Is Desire Built Into The Witness?

Purpose – To "clarify" the opaque witness by either confirming the function of desire that we have attributed to its nature or realizing that desire is not inherent in the witness at all.

Objects needed – A chair. A very quiet room.

Setup – Sit quietly in the chair. We will inquire into whether desire is intrinsic to awareness. Think about a time when there might have been no world and no arisings. And then arisings began.

The Experiment – Begin with the Heart Opener.

1 As you do the Heart Opener, you stand as witnessing awareness. Let a desire arise for the entire world to be different in some way. Let the desire become vivid and intense if it seems to be going that way.

2 Now check – is there anything about this desire that makes it part of the nature of yourself as witnessing awareness? If it is really part of witnessing awareness, then can you still be witnessing awareness when this desire is not present?

3 Or is this desire an appearing object arising in awareness? In this case, you are still witnessing awareness whether this desire arises or not. Its presence or absence does not change what you really are.

4 Sanity check 1 – in addition to the desire that just arose for a different world, do you experience or intuit *another* desire that is built into yourself as witnessing awareness?

5 Sanity check 2 – in addition to the awareness that you are standing as, do you sense or intuit *another* awareness that has desire as part of its nature? Probably not, but we need to check!

Further Inquiry

You can repeat this exercise by looking for other mental features that awareness might have, such as boredom, free will, choice or the intention to make humans wake up and discover their nature. If these features are really built into the witness, they should be discoverable when you look into the depths of experience. But are they? Or are there in fact many times that no desire, boredom or other state is present?

And even if these features are present, they are nothing more than arising objects like "green" or "itch" or "2+2=4." As arisings, they can't be structurally built into witnessing awareness. They can't be part of its functionality.

You can also repeat the experiments we did while inquiring into the mind. This time, apply them to awareness. Does awareness have any intrinsic properties other than seeingness?

Next, let's look at another important aspect: causality.

Creation And Causality

When we think about things being caused and then about awareness, it can get a bit overwhelming. Causality is a very sticky notion, in that our tendency to attribute causality to things is pretty deep-seated. So when we start thinking about witnessing awareness and all the things we may attribute to it that make it opaque, causality naturally comes up. In this case, there are three main possibilities, and we'll do an experiment with each one:

- Does awareness have a cause?

- Does awareness cause arisings?

- Does an arising cause an arising?

Experiment 28a – Does Awareness Have A Cause?

Purpose – To "clarify" the opaque witness by discovering whether it has causality built into it in some way.

Objects needed – A chair. A very quiet room.

Setup – Sit quietly in the chair. Think about witnessing awareness and what might be responsible for it.

The Experiment – Begin with the Heart Opener.

1 Normally, when you experience something seeming to have a cause, you are able to theorize or actually observe how things were before that object came into the picture. Try to do this with awareness. What is your direct experience?

2 Do you directly experience a situation before awareness, without awareness, anterior to awareness?

3 Do you directly experience the causal process of awareness coming into being? Is it like an egg hatching or a sprout growing into a flower?

4 Do you directly experience brain cells or subatomic particles bringing awareness into being? If you are able to do this, it means that you can directly experience the brain cells or particles without awareness there, and at some point they bring awareness into the picture.

5 If you can do what is suggested by (2) – (4), how is this being accomplished without awareness? Your very direct experience is a case of these images appearing in witnessing awareness. Even if you experienced an awareness-less situation in which awareness was absent, and was then brought into being through a causal process, this experience is awareness itself. How can this happen without awareness being anywhere present?

What we are investigating is this. If awareness is something that somehow *arrived on the scene due to a cause*, then how did it get there? Was there a cause for this? If so, then what kind of cause can it be, and how can it be known that a cause is really happening? After all, according to this causal narrative, awareness isn't even present yet. In general, how is this supposed to work?

Experiment 28b – Does Awareness Cause Arisings?

1 "Watch" a few arisings appear. They will come and go. Focus on a particular arising as it comes up. Did you directly experience this arising to be produced by witnessing awareness? For you to directly experience a causal process here, it needs to be more direct than the speculation, *"Well, it must have been caused by awareness. Where else could the arising come from?"* Look for a directly experienced causal action, link, movement, force or some other connection between awareness and the arising.

2 If you are able to directly experience a causal influence, what did it look like? Describe it as precisely as you can. Isn't this object itself an arising? If so, then it is in the same position as the arising you tried to find the cause for. This new cause-arising is just another arising needing a cause from within awareness. (For the case where the cause of one arising is supposedly another arising, see the next experiment.)

3 Even if you could identify a cause of an arising, does this allow you to predict or control future arisings? Often, causes are supposed to be able to do this. Think of the gardener who can use water, seed and fertilizer to cause a plant to sprout and grow in a certain way. Quite often we think of the causes of our experience like this too. We seek a better plant by trying to control and improve how experience shows up for us. We also might think we are getting closer to Awareness by identifying the causes of our experiences. Do you have direct experience of being able to do this with arisings?

Experiment 28c – Does An Arising Cause An Arising?

When we think of causality, arisings and consciousness, this is the most common situation. This is where we feel that one arising is caused by another. For people doing inquiry, one of the most relevant and interesting situations is where a certain thought- or belief-arising causes a certain unwelcome emotion-arising. The feeling is, *"If I could only control that causal process, I would be able to prevent unwelcome emotion-arisings!"*

Of course, therapeutic forms like psychiatry and psychotherapy do just this, the same way that gardeners control the health and beauty of their plants by controlling the causes. In everyday life, people communicate with the world and others according to the model of causes and effects. But when we have already realized that everyday life and plants and minds and gardeners and therapists are nothing more than arisings in awareness, then we have realized that the causes and other tools they use are also nothing more than arisings in awareness.

Here, we are investigating at a more profound level. We've already realized that the causes of everyday life are nothing more substantial than arisings. What we are now looking for is the cause (if any) of arisings themselves.

So we will look into the example of a thought causing a feeling.

> *"When I think about all the things that my mother did to bring me into the world and to nurture, safeguard and raise me, a very poignant and loving feeling arises."*

1 Quite often, we seem to experience a thought or thought pattern that is predictably followed by a certain emotional feeling. Try to think of one of these. You can use any example that works for you. I will write this exercise in term of the example of mother's love.

2 Be very quiet. Let the thought(s) arise. You will shortly witness the emotions arise that usually follow these thoughts. Let all these arisings arise, and see them. We will now look for any causes among them.

3 In Step (2), you witnessed several thought-arisings come up, which were then followed by several emotion-arisings. Let yourself remember that this has happened many times before.

4 Among the thought-arisings and the emotion-arisings, did you directly experience any **cause**-arisings? Did you experience a thought-arising that was pushing, pulling, forcing or creating an emotion-arising? Did you directly experience a causal connection? Just what kind of object is it that looks like a cause? Does it come self-labeled as a cause?

5 We are not investigating memory here, so we can use a little of it. You have seen this same pattern many times before. Even if you cannot directly experience an arising that you can pinpoint as the cause of the emotion-arising, is it possible that you are being influenced by the very regularity with which this pattern happens? Might you be saying to yourself,

> *"This has happened many times before. It is too frequent to be random. There is a pattern here. So there **must** be a cause of this pattern."*

In other words, even if arising "a" is always followed by arising "b," does this mean that "a" *caused* "b"? In addition to a certain succession or regularity, do you also directly experience a cause?

6 Check again. In addition to the pattern (which we will examine below), do you directly experience a cause of the pattern? Even if you did, that cause would be another arising, which itself would require a cause. Do you directly experience any arising truly being a cause without another arising making the claim that it was a cause? You still have not directly experienced a true cause....

Patterns

> *My teacher told me that behind awareness there is a*
> *grid that is responsible for the structure we experience*
> *in the world. Awareness is sort of draped over this*
> *grid.*

A student

In a nondual inquiry class I was teaching one time, a student told the class that this was what his teacher would say to explain why we observe patterns. This grid was supposed to be the real reason that patterns appear. It's the "template" idea, like a "paint-by-numbers" where the numbers tell you where each color goes. Once the paint is in place, you can't see the numbers any more.

Arisings always seem to be *this* way and not random or chaotic. In fact, even if we can't find a cause for arisings, it still seems like they arise in certain patterns. They don't seem to be random, chaotic or unpredictable. We feel strongly that if arisings aren't random, then there must be a guiding influence behind these patterns.

Let's look into this more closely.

Experiment 29 – Is There A Pattern To Arisings?

Purpose – To "clarify" the opaque witness by investigating whether there is something within awareness that makes patterns of arisings occur.

Objects needed – A chair. A very quiet room.

Setup – Sit quietly in the chair. Imagine what experience would be if there were no patterns or predictability whatsoever. Would it even seem like there are arisings or "things" in the first place? Also, think about the many patterns that there seem to be in the everyday world.

The Experiment – Begin with the Heart Opener.

1 Do you directly experience anything "inside" or "behind" awareness that is like a grid or template?

2 If you did directly experience a grid or template that seemed to be behind awareness, then this would appear. If it appears, then it is an arising in awareness. Check if anything like this happens in your experience:

(1) Something appears.

(2) It seems pattern-like.

(3) In fact, it seems like a deep structural element hidden in the depths of awareness.

Inquiry

If something like the 1, 2, 3 sequence above occurs, then this is three arisings appearing to awareness. Arising (2) makes a claim that there might be a pattern present, and arising (3) makes a claim that it might be a very important structural element. But 1, 2, and 3 are arisings. As mere arisings, they are not patterns or templates. Is there any part of 1, 2 or 3 that provides direct experience of a pattern, structure or template?

- Day seems to be followed by night.

- Thoughts of love seem to be followed by feelings of love.

- Things fall down, not up.

- When you are standing upright on the ground, the sky always seems to be above the ground. The sky seems blue and the trees seem green, not vice-versa.

Think of all the scientific principles and laws you've heard of. Just because they don't happen randomly, does this mean that there is something inside awareness controlling the outcome? Is awareness like a big air traffic control center? Can you find any control center inside awareness?

Or is it that an arising is attributing pattern-hood to awareness? Would there really be patterns if an arising didn't "claim" so? Aside from the claim that there are patterns, what is your direct experience?

Levels Of Awareness?

Similar to patterns is the idea that there are levels of awareness. Most of these ideas come from some sort of spiritual teaching. This makes awareness seem complicated and opaque, as though it's doing things we would love to understand but can perhaps never figure out!

Here is a quick list of some notions of levels that you may encounter:

- The *Vyavaharika* (relative) level and the *Paramarthika* (absolute) level of consciousness

- *Saguna Brahman* and *Nirguna Brahman*

- The five "sheaths" in Advaita-Vedanta (physical, energetic, mental, wisdom, bliss) and pure *Atman*

- Consciousness with attributes and consciousness without attributes

- Consciousness at rest and consciousness in motion

- The working mind and the thinking mind

- Waking, dreaming, deep sleep

- The opaque witness, the transparent witness and pure consciousness

You will find some teachers who are serious about consciousness having these sorts of structures or layers. And sometimes, the story about levels and layers is a teaching device to help the student in a more bite-size or user-friendly way. This is because if a teaching doesn't use any sort of levels, then the only thing it can use is "final" notions such as "Pure consciousness. Awareness is all. No duality. You are It." If the student doesn't understand this "no-level" teaching, then the only thing it can do is repeat itself.

So the division into layers is a pedagogical device. It is a series of pointers that get more subtle as the student's understanding deepens. At some point, the teachings plan that these very notions of layers will themselves be investigated and seen through. This usually happens at the later ends of the teaching, after these tools have done their job in showing the nonduality between the world, mind and the self. At this point, the tool is no longer needed and can itself be investigated and deconstructed. If the process of deconstructing the tools happens too early, then the tool will lose its ability to deconstruct the world and the mind. If it happens too late, the student might lose interest or confidence in the teaching itself. The teaching might not seem "nondual" enough!

I'm actually glad that tools and models like these are available. In my own inquiry, a few of these models grabbed my attention and drew me into the teaching. If all nondual teachings said only that "awareness is all, period," I wouldn't have known where to begin. It would have struck me as too abstract and irrelevant.

In my case, I needed some sort of hook or handle to get me into it. Many skillful teachings have these hooks, carefully crafted to respond to the needs and presuppositions of those inquiring into the truth. And the same teachings are able to deconstruct their own hooks. So it's pragmatically effective for teachings to have these notions of levels and layers, especially at the beginning and middle stages. It's OK and even helpful for the student to provisionally glom onto some sort of structure as an actual feature of reality. I glommed onto several of these in my own inquiry.

But by the end of inquiry, none of this should be left over. You use a thorn to remove another thorn, then throw both of them away. You don't regard any of these models as features of absolute reality. As one's understanding and stabilization comes to fruition, one becomes free from the very same models that the teaching used in presenting itself. This goes for the entire teaching itself as well. At best, it is self-erasing. In direct experience there are no levels or layers.

Time And Space

Are time and space built into awareness? Does awareness obey fundamental spatiotemporal laws? Is awareness a chronological thing, with a past, present and future? Does awareness extend to all corners of the universe, spread out farther than the farthest galaxy?

Space

In a sense, we have already investigated space. This was while we investigated the world and the body in Parts 1 and 2. We found physical objects to be nothing external or independent, but to be arisings in awareness. We found the division between "internal" and "external" to be a notion which is also an arising in awareness. We actually did not find anything to construct space out of, and nothing to divide it with. We never directly experienced physical extension, and never experienced the universe as a physical container inside of which there are present or absent objects.

Without any actual physical objects taking up space or being physically extended, we don't need to have external physical space. Where did this idea of space as a huge container come from? It was from Western science. Early in 1687, Isaac Newton was the first to posit a notion of "absolute space."

> *Absolute space, in its own nature, without regard*
> *to anything external, remains always similar and*
> *immovable. Relative space is some movable dimension*
> *or measure of the absolute spaces; which our senses*
> *determine by its position to bodies: and which is*
> *vulgarly taken for immovable space ... Absolute motion*
> *is the translation of a body from one absolute place into*
> *another: and relative motion, the translation from one*
> *relative place into another...*

Philosophiæ Naturalis Principia Mathematica

This is the granddaddy of all container notions. For Newton, absolute space is like an unmoved container that doesn't depend on physical objects or an observer. Relative spaces occur within absolute space and depend on an observer.

But the notion of absolute space was controversial, even in Newton's own era. Philosophers such as George Berkeley and Gottfried Leibniz discarded the idea, arguing that without bodies or some other frame of reference, absolute space just didn't make sense. More recently, one of the revolutionary innovations of Einstein's theory of special relativity was that space (and time) depended upon an observer.

Our inquiry goes in this same direction, as we discover that what purports to be objective is never experienced as truly objective. No object or phenomenon is ever directly experienced to be separate from awareness.

Specifically, by this point, we have discovered that there is no direct experience of any physical object, and no direct experience of a separate observer. We have also realized that with no borders or edges, there is no experience of containment in the first place. We never experience awareness being "inside" space, because we never experience a border "outside" awareness. (We never experience a border "inside" awareness either.)

With these realizations, notions of space and containment and physical separation simply fall away.

Time

We haven't investigated time yet. Awareness can very easily seem like it is structured by time, because it seems like arisings happen in succession. Experience seems like a serial stream of arisings, occurring one after the other. Or maybe arisings happen in time as sort of an enabling container.

Of course, it's easy to glibly say that with no memory and no evidence of an arising other than the current one, there can be no time. But we still may think that there is something special to time, even if time is not constructed from a succession of arisings. Maybe arisings happen *in time* as a structure that is already there? So time is definitely important enough to deserve its own investigation.

Let's take a very close experiential look into time. What is our direct experience?

Experiment 30 – Is There Time In Awareness?

Purpose – To "clarify" the opaque witness by investigating whether time is intrinsic or internal to awareness.

Objects needed – A chair. A very quiet room.

Setup – Sit quietly in the chair. Without trying to "be nondual" and without doing inquiry, just let the everyday sense of time arise. Let time flow by, however that seems to occur to you in an everyday sense.

The Experiment – Begin with the Heart Opener.

1 Do you experience time in deep sleep? Do you experience time in the midst of being caught up in a sunset or dramatic movie?

2 Let's look at a single arising. Let an arising arise, any arising. While the arising is present, do you experience it moving from the future to the past? Do you experience it moving across a field of awareness the way a car moves across a camera lens? (Does the car even move without another arising saying "it moved"?)

3 Do you directly experience a future arising? A past arising? That is another way of looking into the question: do you directly experience the future? The past? If you do, is your experience anything other than a current arising in the now?

4 Arisings may seem like they occur in a series. You may have the impression that arisings flow by the stationary witness in a succession. But if you look very closely at your direct experience, do you experience arisings passing by? Or is the impression of "passing by" itself an arising?

5 Do you experience witnessing awareness itself to be spread out over time, perhaps like frosting is spread over cake? Do you see awareness extending into the future or past, like a lake extending into the horizon? If you do, is your experience anything other than a current arising?

6 Imagine an arising that seems to be from the future (such as an image in a science-fiction movie) or from the past (as in a historical movie). What is your direct experience of this image? The image may indicate "future" or "past," but is the image in the future or past? Is an *image of the future* really *direct experience of* the future? (Remember back to one of our first investigations where we discovered that a sensation "of" an orange was not actually direct experience of an orange, but an arising in awareness only.) Is time any different from the orange?

Conclusion To The Investigation On Time

Have you directly experienced awareness to be structured by time or to be "inside" time? It is really the other way around. In this experiment, time is nothing more than an arising in awareness. In this way, time is like every other object we have encountered so far – not independent from the awareness to which it appears.

Truth

We have already examined truth in relation to thoughts in Experiments 17 and 18. We saw there that thoughts have no referent. For this reason, thoughts, words and sentences do not point as they are believed to do. Any object, thing, situation or fact that thought can refer to simply cannot be found. Even the thought cannot be found if you look directly. This pertains to words and sentences as well. They have no discernible referents. And if you look for words and sentences in the same way, you won't find them either. Thus the notion of objective or empirical truth stops making sense. It evaporates, as it has no available elements to consist of.

This is also the end of the "truth-effects" that so many theories and discourses produce. You won't be susceptible to these any more. The notion of empirical truth, along with its assumptions and attendant feelings, has dissolved.

How does that happen? At this point in your investigation, you will have looked deeply and intensely for the referents of thoughts, words and sentences. You will have landed on nothing but awareness every time. The same thing pertains to the thoughts, words and sentences themselves. If you look for them, it's just another case of looking for referents and objects. You never find anything other than awareness, and of course, awareness isn't an object either.

Discovering this frees you from truth-effects, which are the feelings and thoughts about how something must be empirically true. There can be a definite landing or grasping or attachment when these kinds of thoughts and feelings come up. But having discovered that there are no referents to any of these things, you are free from truth-effects.

What goes for empirical truth goes for empirical knowledge too. In the everyday sense, if a statement cannot be true, then it cannot be known in the objective sense as referring to a matter of fact in the world.

Truth And Knowledge In The Direct Path

What about the direct-path's references to truth, such as "the truth of your experience"? This is also not an object or thing. It's just an expression that may help prevent an unhelpful way of looking at experience when you do inquiry. The "truth" of your experience is in the directness. When you look directly, you don't use the filters of hearsay, belief, hope, fear, theory or the statements in spiritual teachings that tell you what is supposed to be there. Of course, much of the verbiage in my experiments also seems as if it is telling you what is supposed to be there. But you can test this at any time when you look for yourself. The directness of your experience is the final proof. Your freedom includes this ability to disagree and go a different route altogether.

Knowledge in the Direct Path is also not an object. It is not something to have and to hold. Your knowledge of something is enabled by your discovery of how it is not separate. As you have seen over and over with the experiments in this book, when you "know" something, you really don't know it, but you have rediscovered awareness. It's as though your knowing something takes you home to awareness. This is because in seeking to know anything directly, you always trace the thing to its experienced root, which is the experiencing itself – awareness. This is why you sometimes hear that this direct knowing is nothing other than being.

Conclusion To The Opaque Witness

"Conclusion"; I mean this in two ways. It's the end of this section on the opaque witness and also an indication of how the opaque witness itself dissolves into the transparent witness.

When the witness does anything other than be appeared to, it is to some degree opaque. We have just examined most of the common additional things that we attribute to the witness and found them not to reside there. They include doing, wanting, planning, causing, having levels, being temporal, spatial, knowing and telling the truth.

We tend to personify the witness (which isn't even a thing in the first place). We tend to think of it along psychological lines. In turn, we hope it can explain things for us and provide for us. The opaque witness is a psychologized witness, a lot like the mind of a person.

But the clarifying insight is very simple and moves us towards transparency. Once we have gone through these investigations, we realize that these functions are not built *into* the witness, but appear *to* the witness. When we realize this, we see that these functions appear in the foreground instead of being built into the background. So the background becomes transparent. We no longer imagine hidden things there.

The Transparent Witness – The End Of Suffering

The witness has become transparent when you no longer attribute to the structure of the witness things that appear to the witness. You have correctly distinguished background (the witness) from foreground (arisings). You no longer think the witness is personal. Any sense of a separate self is nothing more than an arising, with no separate owner. And there may just be no sense of a separate self in the first place.

Experience is now a sweet, loving, inviting flow of "this," "this," "this," with no coming and going, no life and death, and no suffering.

You see that no arising can block or overturn the sweetness that is the source and nature of all arisings. There is no suffering, because you see that there is no way that anything can be "suffering" without a label, which is another arising. There is also no place for suffering to reside. There's no desire to improve arisings, no thought about future arisings, and no comparison of arisings. There are no states. You no longer think the witness performs functions, makes plans, has desires or causes things to appear. Here are some other indications that the witness has become transparent.

- You no longer suffer; things seem light, sweet, smooth and flowing. You no longer think of yourself as a person who has experiences and has a stake in getting better experiences. You are open to all experience, to all arisings, because even protests against arisings are nothing more than arisings, so they cannot truly protest. There is freedom and joy in this.

- You don't wish for experience to be different – this notion no longer makes sense.

- Witnessing doesn't seem like a mental state, but rather it seems to be YOU.

- Witnessing doesn't seem as though it's reversible or able to be "lost."

- Witnessing doesn't seem as though it needs practice or vigilance.

- Witnessing doesn't seem like it is happening "here" as opposed to "there."

- You no longer wonder whether awareness should allow one person to see all of another person's thoughts.

- There don't seem to be unseen arisings.

- The witness doesn't seem to be the kind of thing that plans, desires, acts or causes things to happen.

- The witness doesn't seem to have internal regions or partitions.

Unconditional Love And Sweetness

To love is to allow, include, to be hospitable. Awareness, as the very being of you, is open to all that arises. There is no velvet rope or Saint Peter's Gate in awareness. You never block or deny any arising. There are no conditions that arisings must satisfy before they arise. There's no vetting, background investigation or review. All is free to arise in you, as you.

This unconditional love is unburdened. It isn't governed by any rules or moral commandments. This freedom is sweet and open. You are free from suffering, entitification, past and future, coming and going, and free from life and death.

You Can Close The Book Now

> *The witness is the highest limit to which one can go, on the way to the Ultimate. When you reach the [transparent] witness, your understanding it as the witness disappears. But what appeared as the witness continues still, as the Reality.*

Notes on Spiritual Discourses of Shri Atmananda,
Vol. 2, p. 159, Note #906.

If this is really the truth of your experience, then you can close this book! Over time, the transparent witness will dissolve into pure consciousness. "When you reach the witness, your understanding of it as the witness disappears." There is nothing more you need to do.

This will happen on its own. Or if you wish, you may inquire. I inquired. Not because I wanted to be "done," but because I was warmly curious about the infrastructure of the witness – the witness seemed like my experience, but I was fascinated, intrigued actually, by the fact that it wasn't nondual. There was a sense of a great discovery lying in wait. It was like the greatest treasure hunt I'd ever imagined! That was just "me," if you know what I mean. Your mileage may vary. Of course, this inquiry, like the automatic happening on its own, will not occur unless the transparent witness has actually been reached.

It probably can't be over-emphasized that there really is no witness. It is not an object, a level, a state, a viewpoint or a slice of subjectivity. It is simply a designation that summarizes how you might think about your experience. But if your understanding of your experience is that you are the witness, then even though this is sufficient for freedom, it isn't the last word.

The transparent witness dissolves or collapses in the most peaceful and benevolent way because it is not only free of suffering, but it is also inherently unstable. The instability comes from a subtle duality, the distinction between seer and seen. Sometimes this is called the "subject/object duality." This distinction has been present all throughout your inquiry, but it probably hasn't been noticed because so many other issues were occupying center stage.

The Subtle Duality Of The Witness

The seer/seen duality of the witness works like this. In any appearance or arising, no matter how subtle, there always seems to be that **which appears** and that which it is **appearing to**. Or in terms of arisings, there seems to be that **which arises** and that **in which** it arises. You, as the unseen seer, seem to somehow be more intimately connected with the subject of these appearances than with the appearances themselves. It is easy to feel that **I am the seer**. But it is more of a stretch, and may take reminding that **I am the seen**. Both turn out to be true, and can be "proved" through a bit of inference. But there is a felt difference between the two "sides" of an appearance even if we are sure that they should be the same awareness.

So even though the witness is unutterably sweet, it is still character-ized by this duality. In fact, the seer/seen duality may be the most subtle and gentle of all dualities that you encounter on the Direct Path.

The good news is that the seer/seen duality is also unstable. It con-tains the seeds of its own dissolution. By the time you have reached the transparent witness, you will have seen through lots of other dualities. You will have grokked the pattern that has established itself during the course of your inquiry: upon investigation the object always dissolves into the subject. And the only subject there is, is awareness itself.

So now, after you are established in the transparent witness, the seer/seen duality is the only duality in town. The momentum from all the inquiry you have done will sort of carry you through. Objects have absolutely no role to play other than to appear and subside. There are no hooks keeping objects in place. You have no stake in the presence or absence of objects. The seeming infrastructure of the witness is simply not needed, now that the witness has done its work, allowing you to see through all the other dualities. It will dissolve sooner or later.

And if you inquire into the witness, it will also dissolve. It might collapse in a more unexpected and precipitate way. Either way, whether you inquire or life is just lived, the infrastructure of the witness will not be around forever.

This is why you can close this book right now!

. . .

Inquiring Into The Witness

If you inquire into the witness, it will fall away only if the transparent witness has been established. But how would you ever know something like that? How can you be sure? Here I will repeat what I said above about the indications that the witness has become transparent:

- You no longer suffer; things seem light, sweet, smooth and flowing.

- You don't wish for experience to be different – this notion no longer makes sense.

- Witnessing doesn't seem like a mental state, but rather it seems to be YOU.

- Witnessing doesn't seem as though it's reversible or able to be "lost."

- Witnessing doesn't seem as though it needs practice or vigilance.

- Witnessing doesn't seem like it is happening "here" as opposed to "there."

- You no longer wonder whether awareness should allow one person to see all of another person's thoughts.

- There don't seem to be unseen arisings.

- The witness doesn't seem to be the kind of thing that plans, desires, acts or causes things to happen.

- The witness doesn't seem to have internal regions or partitions.

In addition, you can look at why you wish to inquire into the witness. You can ask yourself the following questions:

- Am I somehow dissatisfied with waiting for the witness to dissolve on its own?

- Is there a chance that I am looking for something to gain or accomplish through this last inquiry?

- Does something feel unfinished?

- Do I feel any impulse to make an announcement about my progress, or to compare myself with anyone else?

If any of these reasons lie behind your movement to inquire into the witness, then there is still something to gain or defend. The transparent witness, which consists of your having seen through anything that can be gained or defended, has not been reached. The *opaque* witness may well have been reached, but inquiry has not yet come to its conclusion. More inquiry might do the trick, and you may well inquire into why it's important to have the witness collapse right now. This collapse is the sort of thing where wanting it is actually counterproductive!

This of course brings up the question, "So what kinds of reasons are the good ones?" That is, how do you know that your inquiry into the witness is not motivated by something to gain or defend? In a nutshell, you will know you don't have gaining or defending motivations when it totally won't matter what happens in this inquiry. You will be benevolently indifferent about the outcome. Nothing practical or momentous will seem tied to this inquiry. You won't feel spiritually status-conscious about it. It won't occur to you to compare "your" states with those of other people. Inquiry will feel sweet, but unimportant.

In my case, I felt drawn to inquire. I had no idea about outcomes, and I wasn't in a social context where I traded stories and experiences with other people. I felt drawn by a sweet, strange radiance surrounding the anomaly of the witness. The anomaly was that I was free of suffering and anguished yearning, but the gestalt of "arisings in awareness" was not nondual. My understanding seemed inscribed by a gentle, harmless duality. I didn't know whether this could be resolved, and nothing depended on this inquiry. It totally lacked any goal. But I did feel a wonderful bloom of warmth around the question, and I naturally became oriented to it.

So you may not even be able to isolate a motive for your inquiry into the witness. It is an orientation as goal-less as it is sweet.

Actually Doing The Inquiry

Inquiring into the witness is just more of the same kind of inquiry we've been doing all along. It's like sweeping up a room. First we swept the dust from the whole floor into a single pile. Now we will pick up the pile. It's much easier this way. But even if we don't do this, our pile of dust will get blown away sooner or later, so our inquiry is not urgent.

So let's take a very close look into the witness itself.

Experiment 31 – Can You Find An Arising?

Purpose – To inquire into arisings themselves as we inquired into other objects. Can we find them? Does there need to be seer and seen at all?

Objects needed – A chair. A very quiet room.

Setup – Sit quietly in the chair. Without trying to "be nondual" and without doing inquiry, just let arisings flow by in a sequence of "this – this – this." Get a sense of what this feels like.

1 Let an arising arise. Let it subside. It might seem like the whole world. It might seem like "this," but let's call it (a).

2 Let another arising arise and subside. Let's call it (b).

3 Feel how each one is self-contained and doesn't refer to any other arising. Each is free, causeless and spontaneous in this way; (a) doesn't successfully refer to (b), and (b) doesn't successfully refer to (a). They claim to, but no true meeting is discoverable. There is no true "previous" or "next."

4 When (a) is present, there is no evidence of any (b). When (b) is present, there is no evidence of any (a).

5 In general, see if you can find any evidence of anything outside of "this." Can there be any sensible reference to anything outside of this? If you found any, wouldn't it be automatically included in "this" already?

6 Can you find any evidence of *two* arisings? OK, then is there just one arising? How many ways are there of being only one arising? Does it make sense that one arising happens over and over? No, or else there wouldn't even be a mistaken impression of change or diversity or temporality. OK, then how about one long arising that has never stopped? No, because what makes it an arising in the first place? Does it come pre-labeled as "an arising"?

7 *If there cannot be two arisings, then how can there be even one arising?* To have *one* of something there must be the possibility of having *more than one.* A thing must be a countable thing in order for it to be one of something. But there is no possibility of more than one arising. So arisings cannot be countable, so they cannot be things in the first place.

8 Here is a slightly more radical approach. Assume it is just one arising (we'll examine the problems with this formulation below). With this one arising, just what is it that makes it seem as if it is seen or known? You have discovered over and over what must be required for something to be seen. It must actually be there existing prior to the seeing in order for it to be something that is seen. Is this arising like that? Do you directly experience this "arising" as something existing prior to its being seen? If it doesn't exist prior to the seeing of it, then just what is being seen?

9 *Without even one arising*, how can there even be arisings at all?

10 Can you feel arisings as a gestalt, an understanding or model of awareness, collapse?

Experiment 32 – No Presence Or Absence To Arisings

1 Allow an arising to come up, such as a feeling of presence. Allow it to subside.

2 Allow another arising to come up, such as a feeling of puzzlement (such as *"Where is he going with this?"*). Allow this to subside.

3 In steps 1 and 2, does the arising seem to really be there when it's present? Does it seem absent when it's no longer present?

4 When the arising is absent, is there any direct experience of it? Check for any feeling you might have that seems like a hint of a direct experience of its absence. That is, check for any suspicion that "Hmm, I don't know where it might be, but I know it's not here." If you have this sense, then you have at least a slight notion that arisings can exist outside of awareness. For this to make sense as true, it must be verifiable in direct experience. But can you verify it? If you see clearly how verification is impossible even in principle, then your suspicion will dissolve sooner or later.

5 Can an arising actually be absent from awareness? Without borders, what can "absent" mean? Is an arising like a child in a schoolroom, who raises her hand when she is present, but when she's outside playing hooky she's absent? Isn't the usual meaning of "absent" something like "being somewhere other than here"? In the case of arisings, just where would that be?

6 Can an arising be present in awareness? If an arising can't be outside of awareness, then how can it be inside awareness? Can an arising really be inside awareness without being something separate, closed-off and self-defined in the first place? Can it really be "in" awareness without a pre-designated separate existence, without separate borders and lines of demarcation, like a lump in a milkshake? For an arising, just what would mark it off from awareness?

7 Without presence or absence, how can arisings really be at all?

8 Again, can you feel the gestalt of arisings collapse? It makes no sense to think of them as something seen.

The Collapse Of The Witness

With no distinction between seer and seen, the witness has collapsed into pure consciousness. The model of "arisings in witnessing awareness" is not a true story of how things are at a certain level or stage. And it's not a false story either. Rather, it is a story that naturally leverages the dualistic beliefs and feelings that most people have throughout their lives. We start off feeling pretty sure that there are separate seers and objects seen and feel that the two sides exist across a gap only partially bridged, at best by accurate perception and valid cognition. Instead of denying these assumptions from the outset, the witness model uses them in a skillful way, taking this seer/seen dualism to its most subtle level where it can dissolve.

It dissolves in the very same way that it had helped more concrete things dissolve, such as oranges, hands and feet, and the subconscious mind. We looked for all these things that supposedly existed objectively, and we never found them. We didn't find arisings either. The seeming objectivity of all these things collapsed in every instance, dissolving into awareness.

And so for the witness. When the witness has done its job, it naturally collapses under its own weight into pure, radiant objectless consciousness.

PART 5 – NONDUAL REALIZATION

After the collapse of the witness, there is no longer any sense of duality. It is like sweet, brilliant clarity. Even before the witness collapsed there was no suffering. There is still no suffering. There's also no "no-suffering" as an attainment. There's no sense of separation or multiplicity in experience, and no felt subject/object distinction. Nothing seems to exist or be lost. Nothing seems to appear or disappear. There's no gap or separation anywhere, and no "anywhere" either. There is nothing "here" and nothing missing either. There's no sense of flow either, such as "this ... this ... this."

Here is a longer list of the major dualities that aren't experienced in any way:

- Enlightened/Unenlightened
- Good/Bad
- Light/Dark
- Right/Wrong
- Here/There
- Self/Other
- I/Not-I

- Direct/Progressive
- Success/Failure
- Have/Lack
- Boss/Employee
- Substance/Attribute
- Life/Death
- Path/Life
- Beginning/End
- True/False
- Same/Different
- One/Many

This is not a mood or a meditative state. It doesn't flip-flop on and off. This is not a high-maintenance realization; it's *no-maintenance*. The structures underlying duality have dissolved, and so has the dissolution. Knowledge, love, reality and your very self now coincide in blissful peace and open freedom.

OK, So What's Left?

This is a natural and common question for those inquirers well on their way into the Direct Path. Once people start to see more and more "things" dissolve into awareness, their mind leaps ahead. It leaps way up to (what they perceive as) the finish line. The question is not so much about what to *do* at that point, but about what we'll *have*. People are interested in knowing just what cards will be left on the table. It's actually the old metaphysical question, "After all, what is there?"

So is the Direct Path insistent in saying that it is really Awareness or Consciousness? Does it all come down to this?

There is a short way and a long way to address this question. The short way is this: after nondual realization, the question just doesn't come up. The motivations and structures necessary for this question are no longer in place. When the seer/seen distinction collapses, it takes both sides of the distinction with it. With no more need for appearing objects, there is no more need for that which they appear to. With no more need for awareness that witnesses, there's no more need for "pure consciousness," or awareness that doesn't witness. One simply doesn't feel compelled to land on this. The long way to address this question is through a fresh relation with language (see Joyful Irony below).

Stabilization

Sometimes people report a movement towards stabilization, where the mind and body "catch up." It's as though the mind and body re-frame or re-orient themselves according to your realization.

The old separate "you" is out of the way. Thoughts and actions are no longer predicated on the maintenance and defense of you as an entity. They no longer prioritize you first among entities. You don't take "your future" seriously. You move towards lightness and transparency, while understanding these as metaphors in the broadest sense.

Even in the most everyday terms, the lack of the sense of separation makes for more openness, love, generosity, happiness and wellbeing. You begin to get along more harmoniously with co-workers, family, friends, lovers, bosses and subordinates. You start to treat clerks, shopkeepers, hoteliers, wait-staffers, flight attendants and other service workers without arrogance or a sense of entitlement. You don't get flustered by insults or hateful treatment. You won't harbor ill will against those who mistreat you or your loved ones. Physical pain, injury, sickness and death are not issues but are welcomed in/as the space that welcomes everything else.

Of course, these things are stated in everyday terms. In fact, going back and forth between direct-path terms and everyday terms is an outcome of the joyful irony (see below) in which this book is written! In terms of the Direct Path, you are like the pure radiance of light without a trace of darkness. It's not that you are happy; you **are happiness**. It's not that you are in love; you **are love**.

Can There Be Inquiry After Nondual Realization?

No and yes.

No. There is no more inquiry of the kind that might have been done to assist spiritual seeking.

There is no more spiritual seeking. When nondual inquiry comes to its natural conclusion, there is no more suffering, separation, no sense of "me" versus "not-me," and no sense of metaphysical gravitas. That is, there's no more sense that oneself and other things actually exist, and there's no sense that they fail to exist either. There is no more sense of being blocked from true being or ultimate truth. Dualities have stopped making sense. The old motives of greed and achievement have been pacified.

After nondual realization, none of these things can be motives any more. There is no more inquiry or seeking that has the motive of bringing about peace, wholeness and happiness. These are your moment-to-moment experiences. So there is no more searching for these things.

Yes. There can be inquiry of a different kind. *The motivation is different.* There can be a rich and exciting exploration fueled by different motives such as celebration, curiosity or fascination. One can inquire into different things for sheer joy.

If it makes any sense to say that after realization life goes on, then in that same sense you may continue the association with spiritual teachings. There is no necessity that you abandon them. You may or may not pursue them. But if you do pursue spiritual teachings, your relationship to them has been totally transformed. The difference is, instead of doing these things in order to feel complete, you do them with a sweet passion.

In my own case, after nondual had done its job, I was still interested in spiritual teachings. For most of my life, I had been interested in philosophies, spiritualities, views of life and models of experience. Maybe that's because I grew up in Southern California! So later, while I was seeking, it became quite natural for me to incorporate these same things into my inquiry. I can't say that any of it was totally wasted. When seeking stopped, I didn't lose interest in spirituality. For me spirituality and spiritual teachings were never something I did only as a pragmatic means to relieve suffering. I think that when some teachers say that it's a good sign that you no longer read spiritual books, they have this kind of involvement in mind. The analogy would be that you would stop going to the dentist when your teeth are fixed. But in my case, I also **enjoyed** learning about views of life.

To this day I have actually been reading more and learning more than I ever had before. I became fascinated by approaches to nonduality in different traditions, Eastern and Western. I've discovered many approaches I had never known about before. I have thousands of books on these topics. I've visited more temples and monasteries than I ever did while I was actively seeking. For me it is as fun as it is unnecessary! I have many other interests as well. So if all spiritual teachings vanished overnight, I would be happy doing other things!

Freedom From The Path

We hear a lot about freedom from suffering, freedom from life and death and freedom from limitation. But we rarely hear about freedom from the very path that brought us freedom. Where does this come from and what does it mean?

This freedom is a natural flowering of the freedom from language and conceptuality, as well as the freedom from truth and falsity. These freedoms in turn come from the loving non-referentiality of experience. "Loving" because it is open and not walled off, and "non-referential" because there are no near sides, far sides or objects in experience.

This freedom means that we no longer see any path as objectively true or false, *even the very path through which we realized freedom.* We no longer see any path, even our own, as grounded or authorized by reality. No path is "closer" to things in themselves, or "farther" either. No path gets more points for descriptive accuracy than any other.

This is not a relativism of paths, since when relativists say that "Y is relative to X," they allow Y to change, but hold X as a fixed referent. For example, when cultural relativists say that good and evil depend on culture, they take the existence of "good" and "evil" as dependent on something else (culture). But they don't take the existence of culture as dependent. They allow culture to remain as though fixed and unquestioned. Nonduality has no fixed referents. And it also doesn't mean that anything goes. It just means that after realization we, as a supposed separate entity, are out of the way. We are no longer the pivot point. Actions no longer need to please us. Statements no longer need to agree with us. We find ourselves moving with all, as all, as love.

Having fallen in love with awareness, even before nondual realization, you would not be attracted to a cruel or unjust path in the everyday sense. This is because you are aware that awareness is the nature of all, and not just the nature of your own self. In the everyday sense, your love spreads out and encompasses all, the same way that awareness is itself unconditional love by never refusing any arising.

In this freedom, we can love our path and books and teachers. We can feel drawn to it more than any other. But it's not because we think this love is warranted by the way things really are. We're free from the impression that there is a way things really are. If a fan of our path tells us that our path is more accurate and gets it right more precisely than other paths, we'd say, "Gets *what* right?"

Joyful Irony

"Joyful irony" is like a bundle of freedoms – freedom from suffering, freedom from language, freedom from conceptuality, and freedom from the path that brought you freedom. I call this bundle of freedoms "joyful irony" after Richard Rorty, a great American philosopher who wrote passionately about the "liberal ironist" and who sometimes referred to himself as an "anti-dualist." Joyful irony is a sort of loving, nondual non-dogmatism. The joy is the love, compassion, care and lack of suffering brought about by your nondual realization. The term "irony" is from Western rhetorical studies and refers to the inevitable ability of language to diverge from literal statement. The way I am using the term, "irony" is not the mental attitude in which one may say the opposite of what they mean in order to be cynical or sophisticated. Quite the opposite. The irony in joyful irony is the freedom of thought and language when it is unfettered by notions of realism, objective truth or accuracy. It is freedom from the need to be "right." Joyful irony includes love and freedom from even your own most cherished path.

Joyful irony frees you from disagreeing with others about which path is better, faster, truer and more effective for humanity. It frees you from arguments on Facebook and Yahoo about what is more nondual and what others should do to find happiness. You see that disagreements like these depend on the assumptions about the reality of independent things, ideas and people. And you haven't found any of these, no matter how closely you've looked. You are free from the assumption that we can compare what is said to external "facts" about the world and spirituality. These are all disputations, assumptions and comparisons that the joyful ironist simply doesn't have a taste for.

There is a deep and abiding freedom in joyful irony that opens up to the full complexity and richness of life. You are free to go with the heart. Every path has social, cultural, esthetic and normative associations, whether or not these are part of the path's official teachings. These elements are like the path's lifeway, and no path lacks these elements. Certain art, music, images, tastes, sounds, activities and ways of moving the body are preferred. As a joyful ironist you are free to stay with the path you are familiar with. You may feel joy, love and gratitude towards the teaching and the teacher. And just as much, you are also free to go elsewhere. As a joyful ironist you are free to engage in areas (including other paths) that are not associated with your path. This point seems obvious, but there is a subtlety that makes it very sweet. It is this. Part of the *irony* in joyful irony is the deep realization that one's engagement with anything is not a matter or mirroring or verisimilitude. Your engagement is a matter of heart.

Several traditional paths claim that their particular language wrote the world into being. The joyful ironist doesn't look at these claims as conflicting historical assertions, and doesn't attempt to ascertain which claim is true and which is false. The joyful ironist doesn't feel that the world comes pre-scripted in any privileged way at all. Notions of accuracy or verisimilitude between paths and the world have lost all power over the joyful ironist. And at the same time, the joyful ironist can be joyfully in love with one or more paths.

A path is not a matter of accuracy. It is a matter of freedom. There is an open-hearted thrill and a sweet intimacy in this realization.

Joyful Irony and Language

"How should I say things?" This was a problem I confronted even before the conclusion of nondual inquiry. For most of my life, I had the realist bug pretty severely. Things and my self were very real. I was very concerned with saying true things in the most accurate way. This made me argumentative with others who had different views of things. Whatever philosophy or ideology I happened to like got elevated to the greatest truth of the universe! So this was a sort of pattern that followed me into nondual inquiry.

During my inquiry, the Direct Path seemed as if it told the true and accurate truth of things. In fact, for me, this was part of its power. It gave me confidence in the teaching. If someone had told me about this freedom from paths, I wouldn't have understood it and would have felt disoriented. After all, I was thinking, "How can a teaching help if it isn't telling the true truth!?"

But then I saw through the truth claims made by conceptuality and language. For a while, I sort of felt that I was without a language. I felt what the ancient Greek skeptics called *aporia* (lack of "pores" or ways to get through). I had been so used to the feeling of calling things by their "right" names that I temporarily felt like I didn't know what to call things or even what to say. After a while this melted away into a wonderful, light and loving freedom where a different sort of engagement arose. Language could be used, but I had lost the urge for it to hook up with an independent reality or be authorized by the nature of things. I call this "ironic engagement." One uses language passionately, poetically, creatively and lovingly, but doesn't take it to the bank.

So how should one speak? Again, the short way to answer this is that it's a question that after a certain point in the inquiry just doesn't come up. The joyful ironist doesn't have concerns about questions of accuracy or correspondence between a language and a world outside of experience. That realist model of experience which was associated with so much separation and suffering has become dismantled. The joyful ironist is free to resonate with one or more vocabularies while not being dogmatic about any of them. Another irony is that you are even free to take up an old-fashioned realist vocabulary again. This is a sort of joyfully ironic engagement. It is a direct outcome of your freedom, because you can no longer really "be" a realist.

There are no rules here. Life is lived in freedom. As a joyful ironist, one may gravitate to other paths and other facets of life altogether. One may teach, or not. Some people take up yoga, psychotherapy, art, music, dance, sports – the field is open.

Teaching In The Direct Path

There is a saying to the effect that the teacher is not really teaching. What is really going on, according to this saying, is simply being present, or merely singing like a bird in a tree.

This kind of discourse has its functions. Depending on many factors, it can come across as encouraging, mystifying, or inspirational. It can even be occluding. But it is not the only way that teaching can be talked about.

In some gatherings or in private sessions, teachers in the Direct Path set aside this discourse and talk about teaching in a very open way. They don't insist that "there is no teaching or teacher." Instead, it is deeply understood that the words "teaching" and "teacher" are no different from other words, which all refer to awareness anyway. There is no reason to forbid some words from one's vocabulary while permitting others. So if teachers can mention a shopping trip or an airline ticket, they can mention teaching.

This linguistic even-handedness opens up an unlimited space of freedom in which teaching can take place. Thus far, teaching in the Direct Path has taken place through printed, electronic, digital or online sources, and face to face contact in private sessions and groups. I'm sure that other possibilities will develop. The activities have included dialogues, inquiry, meditation, body awareness, and a full exploration of the world of bodily, mental, intuitive, aesthetic, emotional and intellectual experience.

It is also recognized in the Direct Path that it is one thing to come to the end of one's nondual inquiry, but another thing altogether to present it to others. There are no rules set down about this, but the direct-path teaching is not a talking therapy. It tends to be global and deeply experiential. It involves a wide range of sensations, perceptions, movements, thoughts, feelings, desires, emotions and intuitions. Skillful, seasoned teaching is analogous to skill and experience in other fields. This is probably why most direct-path teachers tend to serve as apprentices in some way before setting out on their own.

Because the Direct Path provides the freedom in which the teacher can actually talk about teaching, good teaching becomes appreciated. In the everyday sense, teachers care about doing a good job, helping the student become unstuck, presenting an inspirational example of the teaching, or showing which insight, movement or opportunity may be most effective. Teachers care about the welfare of the student. The ultimate happiness of the student drives the entire enterprise of teaching. In this way, teaching in the Direct Path has a lot in common with spiritual traditions that are thousands of years old.

There is a very freeing outcome to teaching in the Direct Path. Just as the path ultimately provides freedom from the path, the teacher at some point gently deconstructs the sense of the objective reality of the teacher. The teaching liberates you from the teaching, and the teacher liberates you from the teacher.

ENDNOTES

1. Quote taken from **Notes on Spiritual Discourses of Shri Atmananda: Taken by Nitya Tripta,** Vol. 3, p. 76, Note #1283. All page references are to the three-volume edition of **Notes** published in 2009 by Non-Duality Press and Stillness Speaks. In the Preface, Nitya Tripta has this to say about how this immense work came about:

> *Though I have been closely attached to Shri Atmananda Guru ever since 1927 (when I was accepted as his disciple and initiated), it was only in November 1950 that I made bold one day – at the instance of a distinguished friend of mine – to make an attempt to take some notes on that day's talk, which had been particularly compelling. The friend left the same night. I wrote down the notes the next day and most hesitatingly submitted them at Gurunathan's feet, to see if they could be sent to the friend.*

> *He gladly ordered me to read them and I obeyed rather nervously. He listened to them patiently, and suggested some small deletions to avoid controversy. At the end, he asked me with a luminous smile on his face: "How did you do this?" I humbly replied, "I do not know," and told him the circumstances. He laughed, and said: "I am pleased with them. You may send them to her and also continue the practice."*

> *I realized immediately how I was a simple tool at the merciful hands of the Absolute, and prostrated at his feet. He blessed me with both hands, and I stood up in tears. Thus encouraged and enriched, I continued the practice till the middle of April 1959.*

> *That was how these notes came to be. Subsequently, they were twice read out to Gurunathan [Shri Atmananda] himself, and finally approved by him – as true to his exposition, both in idea and in rendering.*

> *Though intended originally for the benefit of the disciples alone,*
> *who already had received directly from him the fundamentals*
> *of his exposition, they are now printed and published for the*
> *benefit of the general public as well. They have been found to*
> *be helpful to all those who have acquired at least a modest*
> *acquaintance with his method of direct approach to the*
> *ultimate Truth.*

> – Nitya Tripta, **NOTES**, from the Preface, p. ix.

2. **Notes**, Vol. 3, p. 77, Note #1283.

3. **Notes**, Vol. 1, p. 1, Note #1.

4. Some nondual teachings speak about a reality "prior to consciousness." In those teachings, "consciousness" is what the Direct Path would call the generic state of waking and dreaming. And "prior to consciousness" is what the Direct Path calls pure consciousness – consciousness without the superimposition of the witness aspect.

Index

163, 180

Heart 3, 4, 25, 30, 38, 84, 104, 107, 157, 158, 222

Heart Opener 25

Heindel, Max 158

Here/there (duality) 216

Hinduism 158, 171

Homer 120

Hui-Neng (Sixth Ch'an Patriach) 124

Hung-Jen (Fifth Ch'an Patriach) 123

I

I/Not-I (duality) 216

I-Am, the 158

Identification 5, 6, 7, 164, 186

Independence 24, 37, 40, 46, 48, 55, 58, 59, 61, 72, 77, 81, 82, 117

Indignation 16, 87, 88, 171

Inference 27, 33, 209

Inquiry 1–6, 13, 14, 60

Nondual inquiry 4, 5, 6, 24, 35, 63, 84, 127, 197, 218, 222, 224

Insects 155

Internal/external 70, 113

Investigation 7

Irony. *See* Joyful irony

Irony, Joyful. *See* Joyful irony

J

Jagrat avastha (the waking state) 109

Jealousy 8

Jesus 3

Johnson, Samuel 15, 43

Joy 207, 219, 221, 222

Joyful irony 218, 221, 222

Judgment 102, 147

K

Kinesthetic sense 133

Klein, Jean 1

Kleshas 125

Knowledge 3, 4

Koshas. *See also* Sheaths
  Manamaya kosha 158
  Vijnanamaya kosha 158

Krishna 3

L

Labeling 65

Lang, Wei 123

Language 14, 49, 57, 59, 143, 168, 220–222

Lectio divina 2

Leibniz, Gottfried 202

Levels 23, 70, 121, 157, 158, 199, 200, 206

Levels Of Awareness 199

Levy, John 1

Liberation 63, 171

Life/Death (duality) 217

Lifeways 222

Light/Dark (duality) 216

Limbic system 159

Limitation 70, 112, 113, 220

Liquorman, Wayne 164

Literality 143

Locke, John 64

Love 1, 3, 4, 7, 13, 22, 25, 26, 112, 115, 182, 188, 195, 198, 199, 208, 217, 218, 220, 221, 222

Love, unconditional 112, 182, 208, 220

Lucille, Francis iii, 1

P

Paramarthika (absolute level of consciousness) 199
Paris 144, 145, 146
Parrhasius 31
Patanjali 171
Path 5, 126, 139, 140, 167, 205, 218, 220, 221, 222, 224
Path, Direct. *See* Direct Path
Path/Life (duality) 217
Patterns 189, 197–199
Pedagogy 200
Perception 1, 12, 18, 20, 21, 27, 30, 35, 39, 45, 55, 64, 90, 99, 101, 113, 122, 130, 132, 170, 188, 190, 215
Person 2, 4, 5, 6, 12, 13, 14, 21, 22, 24, 29, 38, 39, 45, 70, 76, 78, 83, 84, 96, 99, 100, 106, 109, 114, 118, 121, 127, 143, 147, 148, 158, 187, 206, 207, 210, 211
Phaedo (dialogue by Plato) 100
Phantom limb pain 84
Philip Renard 1
Philosophiæ Naturalis Principia Mathematica, by Isaac Newton 201
Philosophy 43, 56, 101, 222
Physical fitness 5
Physicality 56, 113, 132, 188
Physician 89, 92
Platform Sutra 123
Plato 100, 121
Pleasure 23, 68, 69, 85, 92, 139
Pointing 9, 33, 77, 93, 133, 137, 142, 167
Positionality 92, 94, 95, 114
Postmoderns 21

Pressure 153
Psychiatry 4, 195
Psychotherapy 5, 195, 223
Pure consciousness 10–11, 63, 117, 118, 155, 199, 208, 215, 217, 227
Purpose 1, 9, 17, 85, 171, 177

R

Rand, Ayn 17, 148
Reactivity 11, 108, 111, 112
Realism, Naïve 17, 18, 20, 22, 148
Realism, Representative 20, 21, 22
Reality 12–13, 15, 17ff, 25, 28–32, 60ff, 64–67, 74ff, 86, 92, 107, 115–120
Reality effect 22, 23, 42ff, 44, 47, 48, 50, 54, 55, 60ff, 62, 63, 91, 92, 116, 144, 159, 171
Realization 8, 13, 58, 103, 109, 119, 120, 142, 170, 217, 218, 219, 220, 221, 222
Realization, Nondual. *See* Nondual realization
Reference 140, 141, 142, 156, 202, 213
Remembering 141
Renard, Philip 1
Representationalism 18
Repression 157
Right/Wrong (duality) 216
Rorty, Richard iii, 221
Rosicrucian Cosmo-Conception, The (by Max Heindel) 158
Roundness 20, 61–66
Rupa jhanas 171

S

Saguna Brahman 199

Y

Z